At the Top of

Also by Carola Matthews
The Mad Pomegranate Tree — An Image of Modern Greece

*At the Top
of the Muletrack*

CAROLA MATTHEWS

MACMILLAN
ST MARTIN'S PRESS

© *Carola Matthews 1971*

All rights reserved. No part of this publication may be reproduced or transmitted, in any form or by any means, without permission.

First published 1971 by
MACMILLAN LONDON LTD
London and Basingstoke
Associated companies in Toronto Dublin Melbourne
Johannesburg and Madras
and
ST MARTIN'S PRESS INC
New York

SBN boards: 333 12754 4
Library of Congress Catalog Card No. 77–35525

Printed in Great Britain by
THE BOWERING PRESS
Plymouth

Contents

List of Illustrations	7
Acknowledgements	8

Part One — The Way to Aiyiáli

1. Athenian Beginnings	11
2. The Mayor's House	23
3. The Gloved Hand	37
4. The Goat's Teeth	52

Part Two — On the Muletrack — 1968

5. The Rhyme and the Reason	67
6. Nature's Priests and Childish Things	79
7. Astypálaia and the Mongrels	93
8. Pirates and Prostitutes	104
9. Jimmy and the Nightingale	116
10. Jason and the Virgin	128
11. Stroumbo and the Animals	142

Part Three — July 1969

12. The Wrong Time	155
13. Our People	164
14. Barnacles	172
15. The *Chora*	179

16. Snowballs	186
17. The Soup-Wrappers	192
18. Karajoz *v.* Odysseus	199
19. Nikolaki's Lunch	205
20. The Siege	213

List of Illustrations

Between pages 112 *and* 113
1. The 'Mayor's house' in Langátha
2. The author looking across Langátha from the Mayor's house
3. Catherine and Jason at Aiyiáli beach
4. Village steps in Langátha
5. Langátha, view from the Mayor's house
6. Irene
7. Stephanaki (left)
8. Costa in his orchard
9. Vassili's wife with Jason and Catherine
10. The priest of Langátha
11. Michali and Vangeli
12. The feast of the Panayía

Map   *page* 10

The author and publishers are grateful to Henry Matthews for Nos. 2, 3, 4, 5, 7, 9, 10 and 12 and to Ianthe Ruthven for No. 11. Nos. 1, 6 and 8 were taken by the author.

I would like to thank all my friends whose conversation and ideas have helped me in my writing, and especially Peggy Glanville Hicks, who first prompted me to go to Amorgós.

Part One
The Way to Aiyiali

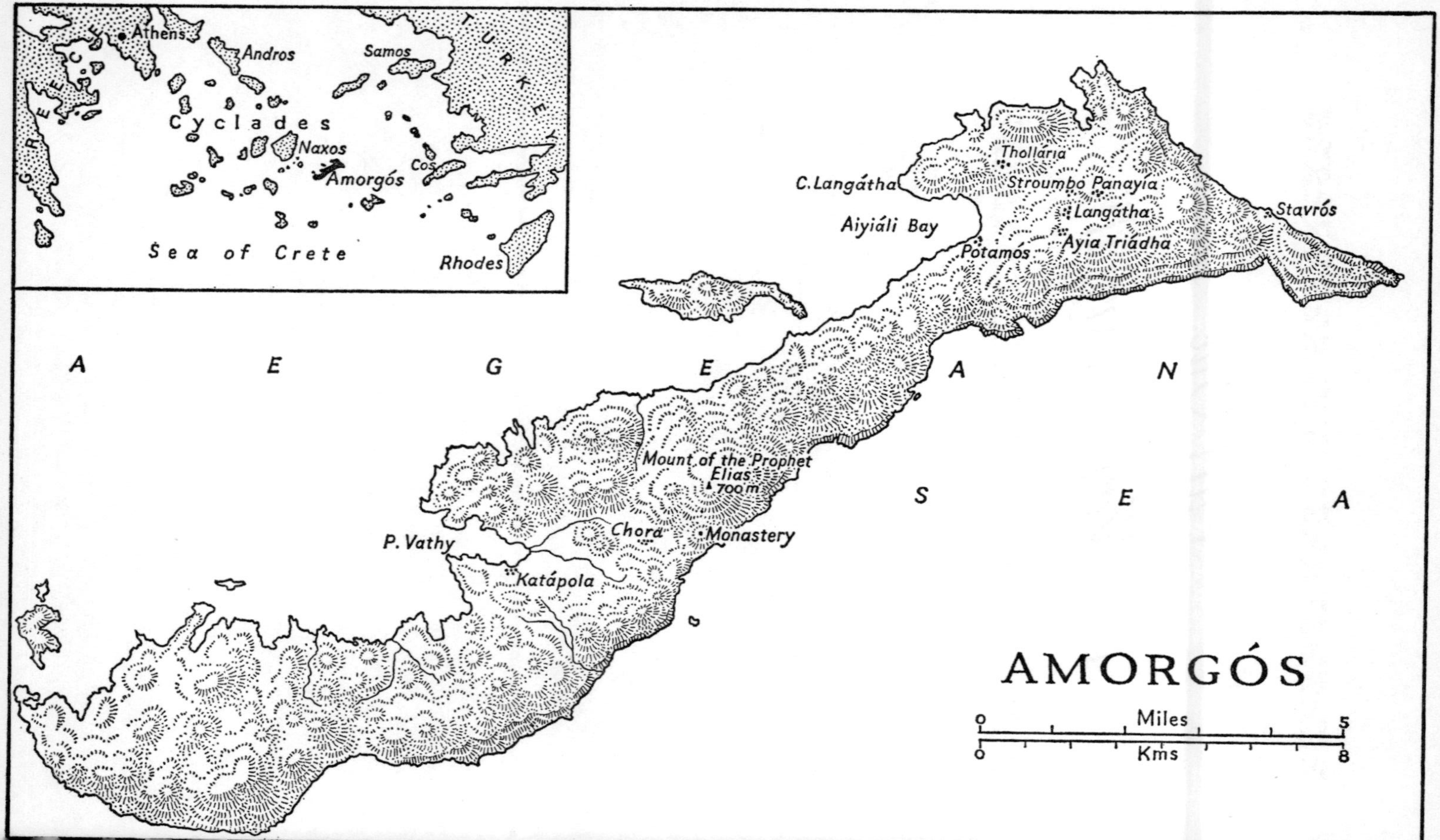
Athens
GREECE
Andros
Samos
TURKEY
Cyclades
Naxos
Cos
Amorgós
Sea of Crete
Rhodes
AEGEAN SEA
Thollária
C. Langátha
Stroumbo Panayía
Langátha
Stavrós
Aiyiáli Bay
Potamós
Ayia Triádha
Mount of the Prophet Elias
700 m
Chora
Monastery
P. Vathy
Katápola
AMORGÓS
Miles
0
5
Kms
0
8

CHAPTER ONE

Athenian Beginnings

AMORGÓS, most easterly of the Cyclades, has been given many names. It has been likened to anything that is serpentine or bony — an eel is appropriate but for its lack of spike. But picture an eel from the air and a dinosaur from the sea, and there you have the first essentials of the island. It lies over twenty narrow miles of the Aegean straining north-east for Patmos and south-west for Santorini.

During the winter, which I spent with my parents in their little Dorset village, the mail van brought in one morning a long roll from New York, and I pulled out from the container an old Admiralty chart of this distant chunk of land. It was 'surveyed by Commander Saumarez Brock, HMS *Bonetta*, 1845 — published according to Act of Parliament at the Hydrographic Office of the Admiralty June 27th 1849', and these terms together with the painstaking precision of the chart seemed strangely grand for such a little-known and unimportant place as Amorgós. It did not seem strange, however, that a friend in New York should have sent it to me in Gussage All Saints, steeped as I was for the season in rural English life. The map was kindly and familiar, it portrayed a place where for two or three months a year I am at home, and if I had been there and shown the equivalent eleven-mile strip of Dorset countryside my sense of recognition would not have been the same.

Relations with places are expressed in arrivals and departures. Sometimes these are sad and lonely, sometimes uproarious. I arrived unannounced and easily on Amorgós this summer, 1968, with senses acute but not emotional. Boats, unlike aeroplanes, allow smooth reorientation, on the water one hovers in a void of non-existence between Piraeus and an island while the experiences of Athens or wherever one has come from are effortlessly shuffled off. The city finally recedes with stumblings down the gangplank, the boatmen's shouts, tightrope manœuvres and heaps of balancing from caïque to landing-stage, and then, when all the people and all their luggage have been sorted into individuals and their possessions and the muleteers taken over, the island is the world. So it was when I landed on the quayside here.

Adoni, whose face in darkness was only two curled bushes of moustache obliterating the gauntness of his cheeks, stepped beside my white mount with quiet grunts of mule language while we moved over the paved track between overhanging fig branches. 'But what will you do?' he asked as we walked into my village. It was eleven o'clock and the houses were falling into sleep. 'We can't wake Costa without waking up his parents, and they are old.'

We opened the gate into the courtyard of my summer house for which Costa had the key and piled up luggage in the recess beneath the arches. 'It's not important,' I said, 'I'll find him in the morning,' and laid out sheets and blankets on the flagstones. 'This is a good bed.'

I had faith now. This is no village to have faith in from a distance, one reason why it is devoid of foreigners, but now I could look up with patient voracity at that closed door on the balcony which for two years I had been waiting to unlock and, visualising tomorrow, feel nothing but happy confidence. The search had been so long to find the place, and yet re-entry could be so casual. I lay down contented and fell instantly asleep.

There was nothing alien to me about those flagstones, there is nothing strange today about single people or groups of people travelling and turning foreign places into homes. Yet I am so often asked, 'Why do you go to Amorgós?' that I feel that I am being called to give evidence on the symptoms of a national disease. I go to Amorgós. I have come to Amorgós. There is such a rightness in my being here that the 'why' hardly needs a question, the 'how' is the important thing.

I talked at length of this last winter with Freya Stark in Italy, and though her house among the foothills of the Dolomites is far away, she is an appropriate person for quotation here as a traveller and a writer of very deep perception who has walked up the muletrack to my house and added her new collection of essays, *The Zodiac Arch*, to the few books on my shelf. In writing and in conversation she has many firmly held views on travelling.

'I have no patience with these restless souls,' she said in tones of disapproval when some young writer was commended to her in those terms as being worthy of her sympathy. Not restlessness but serenity is the quality with which to travel, without that one had better stay at home. And, 'I hate stunts,' she said. Those hairbrained accounts of harrowing experiences in places as mysterious to their writers when they leave as when they arrive have no reason to be written, less still read, for whoever has no knowledge of the language in question can have nothing of interest to report, and adventures are founded on mistakes.

I went a little more than half way with her opinions but asked if she did not like a little madness here and there. She considered, and answered that depending on the circumstances she thought she did like madness, but my generalisation had demanded caution in reply so I gave her an example, 'If you are staying in a certain town or village and suddenly you see a nice-looking bus about to leave for somewhere, is there nothing to be said for the spirit which suddenly leaps on?'

'But if you do that it means that you do not know where you are going and have made no preparation.' Apt to leap off and on myself, I could not answer that.

Without preparation and purpose nobody should travel. Freya herself had recently returned from a fortnight spent in Russia, and her preparation, besides other reading, had been a study of the language for two years. Her motive was serious, her style of fulfilling it — as on all her journeys — serious again, but in the best sense of the word, and who else in her party could have enjoyed the fortnight as she did? Travel with an Intourist group she had to, for this was Russia, and yet somewhere in Turkmenistan she spent the night at a country hotel where only two foreigners had come before, discussed *Sohrab and Rustum* with the manager, and crossed the Oxus on a local ferry boat.

Preparation may smell of the schoolroom or communion, but I have known it anything but solemn. Ten weeks of riotous living in Athens was my preparation this year, for a summer on Amorgós.

Whether fate or oneself is responsible, I cannot say, for well-timed stumblings. 'To stumble' should admit to failure, yet 'to stumble across something' is always fortunate, and there is something reassuring about the conspiracies of life that this happy turn is given to what initially meant putting a foot wrong. I was staying with a friend whom I was helping with a typescript and as I came to the last chapter, without looking for another job, I stumbled on one — only perhaps because I needed it — and immediately, with ten drachmas in my purse, moved into the penthouse of the Litó, a small hotel in the area of Makrianni on the north side of the Acropolis. There I lived precariously and well, always with ten drachmas change, through May and June.

Work was the translation of a Greek guide book into English, my hours were my own to handle, I could answer 'yes' at any moment to a telephone call, 'Carolina, drive me to a ruin or a beach.' Midday blazed on to my terrace where a yard of shade settled beneath my window within arm's reach of the receiver and lengthened in the afternoon, and evenings passed among the taverna chit-chat of the Phengári, 'the Moon' across the road. I had ten weeks of training for the island which I had made into something of a hermitage — what would the preparation be? I like to live my life in chunks, I would deliberately play out my reaction in advance by an excess of opposites. Well, I knew where I was, where I was going and the language. If not highly creditable it seemed to be all right.

'I am a part of all that I have met.' Ulysses was a part of all that he had met. During those ten weeks I thought about his statement very often. I thought about a great many more foolish things as well, but this concerned my being in Athens and my coming to Amorgós. Would not the common traveller more likely say, 'All that I have met is a part of me?' He should have an opinion anyway, for it concerns not me in particular but all travellers. Which is greater, to give part or to take, to lend or borrow, to shed or to acquire? Ulysses was a part of all that he had met. Is it not possible, I thought, to compromise, to claim a two-way system, give and take? Compromise which sounds like a surrender may be the gaining of the best of everything, and everything is a part of something else.

All mountains are built of molehills, and all storms originate in tea-cups. I throw a piece of bread into the sea, and as it hits the surface and a fish appears I am involved in the history of the catching and the caught, the paying and the paid, and each thing that I do of more importance, and every action that every person makes joins in these mechanics, the careering of snowballs which is the history of the world. The Trojan War might never have been fought had not Laomedon cheated Apollo and Poseidon over their payment for the building of the walls. One's life depends upon the side of the road on which one walks. We all know these things and yet we find it difficult to act as if we knew, to see whatever is as vital, or to give a seedling the importance of a tree.

The chunks of action are not neatly severed. I cannot live in categories, I never know what answers to fill in on forms, but rather wish the zest for pigeon-holing life could be confounded. I only know, and all who understand can say this, 'I am a part of all that I have met, and all that I have met is a part of me.'

I did not come to Amorgós to get away from anything, but to have all things with me here, and a violence of living beforehand was to be enjoyed for its own sake and brought along, to be kept with me here at arm's length.

Daily I ached through the translation of my guide book, which I had little business to be doing for I am not bi-lingual, then through many hot and gruelling evenings sat at my employer's office reading back my English into Greek. This was his only way of verifying that I had not made mistakes, and since I was using much vocabulary which I only knew on paper, trying to speak in newspaper language and at the same time convert my tinkerings back into flowery Greek, the method was not infallible. But I paid my way.

'Although Rethymnon has not been able to erase the stamp of the Venetian occupation from its face entirely, it has in modern years been much embellished.' I take exception to that sentence — what is there in Rethymnon to admire but its Venetian fortress? — but there it goes, it pays for my hotel room. Living dots move round the walls of the Acropolis and we are showered with pink and blue emblems of political propaganda. Fortunately the military government have made more headway than any other with rubbish collection in the streets. 'God in his openhandedness has given us freely of these gifts.' The shade begins to move across my terrace, I can venture out and watch the street growing drowsier. 'Long live April 21st!' Out in the country too the slogan had added its welcome to the entrance of the villages:

> Long live the King!
> Long live April 21st!
> Christ has risen!
> Happy New Year!

'God in his openhandedness....' How hot it is today. In May, which mistook itself for August, the villagers went out with the priests to pray for rain, but the drought was long and many crops were spoilt. God perhaps was on holiday or sleeping, and when he realised the subject of their prayers too late did not like to do otherwise but respond in double measure, hurtling us with rain and hail on alternate days throughout the length of June and ruining the later fruits which want nothing but dry sun. 'But,' they say, 'if our weather were perfect what would we be?'

'Gods,' I answered. I wonder if I was right. I wonder even more why they worded the question like that.

'God in his openhandedness. . . .' What am I to do about this sentence to earn a gallon of petrol for my car? For every line I can smoke four cigarettes, for every four lines drink half a kilo of retsina; for the moment I am stymied, fling out my arms in sweating desperation, painfully hit the radiator—God in his openhandedness has turned the central heating on.

I reach for the receiver, 'Concierge, are you mad?'

'Oh,' he says, 'that's all right, we'll soon turn it off.'

He is mad, I must get out and I need petrol. 'God in his openhandedness has given us freely of these gifts which every Greek since the Golden Age has been doing his best to embellish.' My problem sentence requires four words only, 'This is our heritage.'

I've earned my petrol and the telephone is ringing. 'Carolina, you have two letters here, and I've been presented with a bottle of Scotch.' It's Peggy Glanville Hicks. 'I'll be around.' The Acropolis is radiating heat and the owners of the new apartment blocks pull down their awnings. I walk to Erechthíou Street and find the composer of Nausicaa, which had its world premier in the ancient theatre just above us, sweeping the street barefoot. Pink and blue have vanished from her doorstep, and there is a wide parking-space before her cottage walls.

'You remember that note you found on your windscreen, Carolina?' Indeed I do. It threatened to smash up my car if I parked again, though not illegally, in front of her neighbour's door. I certainly remember. Peggy kept it, she knew it would be useful, 'Everyone in my street cuts down their own trees and then parks in the shade of mine. So I stuck the note on someone else's windscreen. It had a remarkable effect.'

She has washed down the patio and her fig shade is the deepest, the coolest in Athens. 'My father was an ex-clergyman — no, he wasn't defrocked, but he wasn't entirely satisfied with God. He used to say, "The world was one of God's early works. Afterwards he improved on it on other planets. If he had had more experience he would have done better with this one." '

Clank — the workmen are out between us and the ancient theatre. I shall write a book and call it *An Early Work*. Clank turns into the stomach-turning horror of drilling and our teeth edge pneumatically until we are jolted into silence. An ancient pavement has been found and for a month the harrassed owner will find his multi-million site declared a sanctuary. Afterwards something will be handed to someone under a table and the drill go back to work . . . doing its best to embellish . . . I've never used the verb so much before.

The groves beneath the Acropolis are littered with contraceptives, and the streets have too few traffic lights. I wait five minutes to brave the unguarded crossing below Peggy's house, composing the first chapter of *An Early Work*, and sleep into the afternoon. The telephone is ringing. 'Are you thinking of excursing tomorrow, Carolina?'

'Of course I am, it's Saturday.'

My friend who sent me the old map of Amorgós, Jim Price whom I have known for years on Mykonos, has come back to teach in Athens and discovered the pleasure of my recent rash of absent-mindedness. We spend a weekend collecting my possessions, a coat, a sweater and a camera, scattered between Megara and Salamis. His beautiful cove on the island of the battle has turned into an area, barred off with prison wire, of festering bungalows, a plague of round brown carbuncles, a hundred on one hillside, a hundred on the next, every one to be mistaken for every other one. We drive in terror round corner after corner, the rash still spreads, and on and on and on. We will not go to Salamis again, we are content as connoisseurs of the rural places of eastern Attica. The guard of Amphiárion, sanctuary of Asclepius, smiles among the pine trees, 'Yes, I am all day alone here with the ruins, but I have the birds. If five nightingales sing in daytime, think how many sing at night.' It is so peaceful here. Poor Pericles, he had no contraceptives and no bungalows.

'Everything is interesting,' says Jim, 'the only difficulty sometimes is to see where the interest lies. If someone is making boring conversation I divert myself by thinking, "Why is this boring? What is not being said?"' We drift in the sea at Skiniá, from two miles or more of white sand and pines, where only our ears are in jeopardy from the bombing at the far end as a pair of jets swoop down with fire on military exercise. 'Go home! It's time for lunch, it's time for your siesta!' Let us absorb full measure of sand, sea, sun and happiness in peace, for next year, or the year after, this beach will be organised.

'It must be,' says Peggy, 'there are too many people. Sooner or later, because of the litter, they must all be organised.'

The Acropolis grows daily smaller, and every day is more marooned. Comb every corner of Athens while it is still ... while still something Athenian remains. Could you not arrange, God, that I could have half a day to see it, not even two thousand, just a hundred years ago? The evening is cool out here on my great terrace, and I dance on its smoothly uneven paving-stones ... 'Which every Greek is doing his best to embellish ...' and take out my papers again.

'Before you set foot on the beach you must judge your strength. "Am I in good humour?" That is the crucial question which needs careful answering.' Oh you hypochondriac Greeks! But I have earned my supper. The Amorgót evening is ending at this hour and the Athenian beginning. The Parthenon turns red. The Persians are attacking!

Across the road at the Phengári the proprietress sits urgently writing her name in patterns on the paper table-cloth. Julia, Julia, Julia. Everything is interesting. What is being left unsaid?

'The people are mad,' cries Gerásimos, 'or I'm a barbarian.' Gerásimos from American Express is the only member of our taverna circle who speaks English. We privately solve the problems of the world, covering cigarette packets and paper napkins with each other's sayings while Julia Julia Julia grows over the table cloth.

'There's no work this year, no work. Four thousand drachmas I pay in rent a month. We are hungry. Where are the customers? Where are the foreigners? Look at me. I am sweeping the floor. Do I hire a woman to sweep?' Her hair is black, a long scar stings down her cheek, she terrifies whichever of her customers do not know that her anger is directed at her subject, not at themselves.

'Not the voice of my heart,' says Gerásimos, 'the voice of my head. . . .'

Julia has burst into dance and the dance into song. She has the contralto voice of the earth goddess, of the matron of Greek tragedy, it is marvellous when directed into triumph.

'When the head and the heart disagree the head is right.'

'Are you in a good humour?'

'What do you say, Carolina? Where are the foreigners?'

The Scandinavians don't come because of the queen. The English don't come because they say they are too poor. The French and Americans don't come because they're in chaos. God was inexperienced and the world is upside down.

'And this girl and I started talking about Chalkís,' says old Panayoti, gaunt in tie and felt hat, laboriously. 'It was the night of Easter Saturday so I said to her, "I'm going to Chalkís for Easter. If we leave now can you get me there in time for the resurrection?" We left at a quarter to eleven. . . .'

Yes, yes, dear Panayoti, but you will confound your legend if you tell the whole taverna about it in detail again. Yes, I did take you to Chalkís for the resurrection and we arrived at the main church five minutes before midnight, yes and we spent eighteen of the next twenty-four hours among Euboian villages, eating lamb and drinking wine, and an old peasant woman in black came out to receive us on her farm and asked me in harmonious and aristocratic English if I could lend her any books on spiritualism, yes and she spoke French and German too, and had known Gandhi in India and worn diamonds.

'So I said to Carolina,' says Panayoti, beginning from the beginning. . . .

'The British communists,' and Gerásimos slaps the table, 'are first of all British and then communists, but the Greek communists are communists first.'

Julia, Julia, far more of a woman, far more attractive in her earthy, earthly way than any of the accepted beauties here, is angry again. 'How stupid we were the other night, we were mad — do you remember? — we turned out the customers before two o'clock and went off to eat ice-cream. From two until five we work.'

'Look at me!' Julia's niece and Saturday-night waitress, Litsa, is innocently ecstatic in the mirror. 'Feel my waist, I go in, I go out, I'm not wearing a girdle, I'm a lovely shape, I'm not a peasant — I'm modern.'

Vassili, the waiter-chef, my gentle friend, half the size of Julia and at all times unperturbed, decides that the customers can wait for him to smoke one cigarette. 'Carolina, come later tonight and —'

No, I am going to bed, I have to finish Crete tomorrow. Give me two minutes only, and one line to write, 'Let me enjoy this moment of brilliance before it turns out to be nonsense in the morning.'

The telephone is ringing before I have woken to decipher the sum of our cigarette-box wisdom. It's Julia at five o'clock. 'Carolina, we want you, will you come?'

The time of preparation is nearly over, the steamer will hoot and I shall go to Amorgós. As this occasion cannot be a precedent I shall throw up my translation and be carried on to saturation point.

The sun has not risen, but as we drive out of Athens it lights up the country road east towards Ráffina. How beloved I am now that I have a car. Julia is too tired to drive and Vassili has no licence. 'Turn off to see my plot of land,' cries Litsa. The hillsides here grow olive groves from Athens to the coast and Litsa has bought a piece of one. 'Look at it! Look at it!' She is leaping in the early sunlight, 'The beauty! Nature! Peace! Wait until my house is built — you will all come and listen to the silence on my terrace. What can you hear? Nothing. Where could you find a plot of land more beautiful than this?'

When the head and the heart disagree . . . Litsa, it is a lovely place, the hillside grows nothing but olive groves and wire fences, and when your house is built it will be in another residential suburb of the capital. Piraeus and Athens were once a city and a town.

'Let's go to Ráffina.' The morning is fresh and fishy, we toast each other over squid and whitebait brought in from the earliest caïques. Vassili, Julia and Litsa are finishing their day, I am beginning mine; we are inside out and upside down and we are a part of the history of the world.

CHAPTER TWO

The Mayor's House

AMORGÓS is like two islands, with villages on each. The Mount of Prophet Elias, a fortress against invaders from the east, rises sheer to seven hundred metres as the summit of the long dividing range. The way between the two chief areas is two hours long for record-breaking fitness, three for continuous hard walking, four for sore feet and five for unsureness of the way. Even the mule track in some places disappears, but in as far as one can walk straight round mountains straightness is the path — eventually one will arrive at Aiyiáli in the north.

This is the poorer region. It has no electricity outside the harbour, and there only during summer when the hotel is open for a maximum of thirty-two visitors. It has no roads, not even for a bicycle. But the capital, the *Chora,* perched beneath Prophet Elias, and Katápola, the port below which faces west towards the parent island Naxos, both have electricity and are connected by a road. There are two vehicles, a taxi and a lorry-bus which negotiates so many bumping hairpin bends while the passengers roll for lack of straps inside that a pedestrian can win the downhill race intersecting its route round every corner on the straighter muletrack. Being the richer area and guardian of the monastery it is the more encouraged by the government. Whatever money goes to Amorgós towards the tourist trade goes there, and if one ignorantly goes 'to Amorgós' by boat it is there that one will probably disembark.

I described my first journey there from Syra and the twenty-hour detour among half the Cyclades in *The Mad Pomegranate*

Tree, then — in the spring of 1965 — a fragmentary manuscript which needed somewhere less distracting than Mykonos to be turned into a book. Did stimulating solitude exist? It sounded impressive, I decided that it must, and by a process of elimination, searching and rejecting, I came to lay my hopes on Amorgós. But after such a sea voyage disappointment is not only less acceptable, it is more likely to befall one than after a few hours' cruise.

I liked Katápola, and that was not enough. It seemed about to rise too fast, while the southern villages were doing the reverse and the *Chora* caught the wind. The monastery, plastered on to its eastern precipice, was one of the most inspiring buildings I have seen, but I could hardly move into a monastery. The fastidiousness of would-be foreign residents becomes more out of hand with every year's experience of the Aegean. 'Wanted, an island with a working atmosphere. Wanted, a white hill village not too far from the sea, where tourist prices have not been discovered, yet not dying. Wanted, an old house with a courtyard, view and water. Wanted, in one spot an amalgamation of all the best things in this sea. Wanted, in fact, perfection.' I did not see it in Katápola.

And yet this island excited me. I felt like stout Cortez about to reach the peak, all ready to look about me in a wild surmise and confronted by a final, thwarting rock. There still remained Aiyiáli as a possibility, and talk of mules or possible caïques became so complicated and concerned with providence that I decided to go the cheapest and — I thought — the simplest way, by foot.

Fortunately a young German anthropologist, Yanni as the island called him, living in the *Chora*, who knew more paths and non-paths on the island than any of the natives, and every rock, whether it was a plain rock or an ancient edifice, ran into me the evening before I planned to leave and said that he was walking to Aiyiáli too. I doubt whether foreigners crossing this part of the island in the last decade have averaged more than one a year, so when I say 'fortunately' I mean that fortune, which often takes an active part in the affairs of men, showed timely co-operation on

The Mayor's House 25

that day. It is a fact which I have never been able to digest that to go from one side of a mountain to the other, even if one's destination is apparent in the distance, is difficult to achieve in any reasonable manner unless one knows the way.

So Yanni was my guide and we walked together, leaving early in the morning and arriving ravenous for lunch. I had something particular to celebrate when we sat down to omelets and retsina, something besides the achievement and the appetite, a moment of recognition which I had waited for for years. That morning after three hours of barren walking, when we rounded the final mountain peak beyond the *Chora*, it came to me, and then surmise was wild.

Small in stately setting, three white villages look over the bay's circumference from high stations on the inside of the cliffs which seem, when they were flexible, to have been curled round for protection to keep the harbour water calm whatever might be going on outside. Aiyiáli, the wag in the island's tail, is Santorini inside out. Walk over the back of the mountains at any point and you look down sheer at jagged sea from suicidal heights. The plain inside is sheltered, symmetrical, and full of olive groves. Terraced fields cover every space between the gorges and every angle less than forty-five degrees.

The look and the recognition are all very well, but they provide neither village nor house. Only the first half of the search, for island and region, was achieved. And yet in an early work this was clearly one of God's successes, and another of his best arrangements was this diffusion of our character, that somewhere each person has a place and style if he can find it, and in each case that place and style may be different. My sense of recognition had been no one else's, there were no kindred spirits teeming here. This is well done, I thought, but this being so, how can each person find his place? He can. He must only listen for as long as need be, wait patiently, be observant, keep in tune until he slides into position, and this is the opposite of escapist travel. He can.

If this were my place I would be free of doubt, but I had already rejected the first village, Potamós, 'the River', which we passed through on our long descent and rejected the harbour over lunch. Potamós in tumbling white on a steep mountainside is in guidebook language 'picturesque' but was it perhaps also a little sad, too far advanced in the process of decay? Forbidding, I thought it, and the title seemed harsh, and yet I felt, 'This village is forbidding.'

The port meanwhile, first to receive Aiyiáli's visitors, was somehow lacking in entity or self-possession, though kindly around its unpretentious harbour-bar with one new hotel, three *cafenia*, one of which is more or less taverna, another less than more, while the third combines itself with telegraph and post office haphazardly functioning in a corner beside the coffee drinkers. But above us the mountains swung around, and on the right Langátha, 'the Gorge', and facing it across the plain Thollaría were still to be explored, and these were villages in their own right.

Have no fear of domestic claustrophobia in Aiyiáli, it would take the best part of three hours to encircle both these villages, climbing down finally from Thollaría to the far end of the long, narrow, sandy beach and back to the harbour for the night. Yanni had business in Langátha and would stay there; I, who had to catch the early-morning caïque back to Katápola, would go on, and only the remains of this day could further the next stage of my search. Aching from the morning we moved on.

The way to Langátha is a paved mule-track through olive groves, a stairway among fig trees beneath a precipice, in the middle of which a crazy white patch is the little church of Ayia Triádha, the Holy Trinity. It winds and breaks up and turns and climbs, and is wide. Thirty minutes bring you into vineyards — someone lives then in this half-tamed landscape — and a mass of white roof rises into view. 'We haven't arrived yet,' said Yanni, 'this must be the longest village in the Cyclades.'

Over two hundred steps led us up to the *platía*, some deep and shallow, others a one-pace staircase narrowing as the houses press together, painted with whitewash doodles, turning beneath an archway, splashed with the glimpse of flower and shrub through doors half open into busy or sleepy courtyards, and we were at the top.

I stayed in Langátha barely half an hour. We drank coffee with the policeman, and one or two people passed by and said this and that. Houses there would be without question for nobody came to this village — some stayed, some left. No one was questioning, no one ferocious, nobody formidable in staring or welcome. Yanni started me on the rough way towards Thollaría and I hurried on to complete the circle before dark. I did not hurry for any other reason, for sure recognition needs no verifying and I had stood in the *platía* of Langátha and felt at ease.

Aiyiáli waits. Mykonos is clinging. I kept the first in mind and went to the island which I knew, and meant to leave and did not. Nothing is so troublesome in searches as ourselves, when the hand that makes a discovery falters and bungles its move. All people can do the searching, but not everyone can grasp. So the summer passed and I went back to England, and the next spring came only with the intention of the year before.

In the meantime I had had an idea worthy, I considered, of the financial cunning of a Greek. My brother, who had introduced me to the country in the first place, an architect who had talked from time to time of the pleasure there would be in possesing land there or converting some old house, was lecturing now at Washington State University and would surely have some dollars spare to make a small Aegean investment a reality. It was years since we had raised the subject, but I decided peremptorily on his frame of mind. What an advantage it would be for him to have an agent to do all the work, a caretaker for one whole summer, someone to lavish care and buy some basic furnishings. So I wrote to him, and he said that five hundred dollars could be raised for a house on Amorgós, of which he sent one hundred in advance.

I crossed into Greece from Turkey through the Dodecanese that spring, and on the way to Mykonos, where I planned to spend one month and no more, found that two hours at Aiyiáli could be fitted in for reconnoitring. It was a poor allowance; I had meant to stay a few days there and settle on a house, but I could not ask a captain to change his timetable. However, two hours between boats is long enough to ask a hundred questions, even to run up the paved way and pant into Langátha, 'Has anything here changed?'

The people smiled.

'Shall I find a cheap house in the summer for sale or rent?' They laughed. Renting may well lead to buying and is a practical first step.

'You can have half the village,' they said. 'You can buy a house for two hundred dollars and a good one at that.'

The inhabitants of the quayside improved upon the story. 'Bah! You can have one for free.'

And still what comes in reach is difficult to grasp. Only the serious position of my typescript, which had turned decisively from novel into travelogue and had an agent and an autumn deadline kept me in tune with what I wanted, and then only in the last days of July did I cease prevarication, abandon familiarity and friends, and unload one night on to the quayside of Aiyiáli such quantities of luggage as made me feel a little foolish as the single foreigner.

In the small-scale hurly burly of the harbour I asked, trying to look inconspicuous, for a room. 'Michali!' someone called, and within five minutes my luggage and I were loaded on a mule. Where was I going? This was no moment to ask, and hardly to wonder, for in such circumstances one is doubtless going somewhere and the answer will reveal itself. The mule trod carefully over the stony end of the long beach, steadily away from harbour noise and lights, on to firm sand as I could tell only from the feeling, unable to see nearer than the stars. It turned inland, we were riding in an orchard, several white rectangles became apparent in the darkness and we stopped at a one-room cottage, a clean box by a pear tree with a table, chair and bed, and Michali lit a lamp and filled the water pot.

Listen to the music, take what is given; the next morning when I woke up in the sandy, seaside orchard, found tomatoes growing at my doorstep and saw Langátha white above us in the mountains, I thought, 'When I am living in the village it would be nice to have a midday cottage by the sea.' I had little money but my brother's hundred dollars and that was not to be embezzled — no, I had broadcast that among my friends to make myself quite certain, I would not embezzle Henry's dollars. But when I passed Michali on the beach that day or the next I discussed the long-term rent as a preliminary to what I had in mind.

I could see that he had children, I knew without doubt that he had children. Wrinkled at forty or a little younger he had a hard-working, healthy father's face. 'Yes,' he said, 'I have four daughters,' and I knew what line to take.

'Do you want one to learn English?' Four daughters, I was thinking, that means four dowries, and he has no son to help. All his working life and his ambition must be centred on the girls.

'Yes, Irene is just twelve and she should learn.'

Rooms and lessons are a good exchange, we hardly had to say it, we did not waste our time on details. Michali and his family lived in Thollária, I was aiming at Langátha, and in the daytime his orchards would be our meeting place.

Establishment on the beach was a frivolous affair compared with serious house-hunting in the village. A beach, be it on some deserted rock, is tourist ground, and this crop of long white bungalows in Michali's orchard had been built for letting. In Langátha meanwhile everything is simple; the people get up early, go out to their fields, come back at dusk, sometimes drink wine, sometimes dance, and sometimes go to bed at nine o'clock. Everything is simple and the simplicity is baffling. I wanted something of it which it had and did not know about.

Here is a village with many empty houses, and on one side, sloping down the mountain, ruins which make me think that if I were an architect I could not go to sleep for working on conversion plans. Here am I, a foreigner, willing to spend a little money, climbing over walls, poking my head through windows, sweating up and down the two main streets or stairways, asking innumerable questions and being thwarted. Houses in such a village are unoccupied for two reasons, one that they are used as store rooms and the other that the owners are away. I had known this, I had foreseen the second trouble, one reason why I should have paved the way more firmly in the spring, but surely in one whole village there must be exceptions, or relatives with authority to act.

'We could move out the potatoes and put you in this room,' one woman offered.

'But I want a house. I want to be able to walk from room to room without walking through another person's entrance.' They could not understand me. How can one person need a house?

Again, 'Whose house is this?'

'The owner is in Athens.'

'Would he sell it?'

'No, it is his daughter's dowry.'

'And this house?'

'The owner is away in Athens. He keeps it for the summer months.'

The inhabitants of Langátha were charming, polite and not over-curious. They addressed me in the second person plural and did not ask how old I was. They were all I could have wished for but that none would provide me with a house.

Nor did the village seem now as empty as it had looked before, rather it had a lived-in air, more cheerful and more lively than the *Chora*. Almost everything inhabitable seemed to be inhabited, and a ruin may be beautiful in theory but is unpractical for the immediate production of a book. On the first day I discovered that the one acknowledged room to let was occupied, and went down to the beach again without even a home base for my search. What I needed was adoption, for in villages, where everything is done by word of mouth, one goes furthest under native wing. On the second morning I was adopted in a back-street wineshop, and of the group of ten o'clock retsina drinkers it was the most unlikely figure that rose to leave with me.

Square-faced and peculiarly blank, sixty-year-old Marco said that he would help. Very slowly, silently, he led me up to the *platía* to his own shop, square and blank like he, with chairs that were seldom sat upon and tables seldom used. 'The shop', *to magazí*, is the term given in villages to the place which provides anyone with what can be provided, or as far as possible what anybody wants, to the grocery that serves drinks, to the *cafenion* that keeps wine as well as the usual coffee, ouzo and liqueurs, that opens a tin of sardines or fries an egg. The farther from the beaten track you go, the farther you go from categories. Marco's shop was everything except a grocery, but that his everything — being in small demand — proved sometimes more like nothing.

'We have a room,' he said. 'My wife will come and she will show you. Then we will find a house.'

He made two cups of coffee and reverted into silence, without further suggestions or ideas. Sometimes I have found it difficult to see a reason for his initial action and can only put it down to basic goodness, which seems in its most inanimate form to occupy a large place among the qualities for which there is space in his mentality. He had no sense of foreign glamour, nor of curiosity. He was not mercenary. He went down in the evening to collect my luggage from the beach by mule, and when he made up my two-day bill — about five shillings a day for dinner, bed and oddments — forgot that heavy chore. He remained a half-dumb, paternal spirit throughout my village summer, and his gentle wife Kyría Mouska accepted accordingly the maternal role.

With the advantage of a village bed and my status improved by new attachment, I continued to search Langátha by myself. And then I found a turret, a disused pigeon house turning a bend between street steps into a tunnel, overspanning it with wooden rafters, crumbling with a maze of outbuildings and a small garden full of hens. It stood in a clutter of other cottages, but overtowering these, unwhitewashed, needing occupation, looking down towards the sea. The owner was in Athens, they informed me, but it was for sale and his brother had the key.

I stood on the terrace half an hour later wondering how quickly I could sweep out the decrepit age inside, put in a table and get down to work. 'Are there houses in the village unoccupied?' They had laughed down at the harbour, 'As many as you like.' Now after two days' frustration this one possibility excited dying hope. The owner's brother smiled beside me saying, 'It's a good house. It needs a little work but you will like it. No, I don't know how much my brother wants, but I'm going to Athens on the boat this evening, so I'll ask him and let you know.'

'And when will you be back?'

'On Friday.' That was in four days.

The improbability of my meeting him on the very day of his departure encouraged my conviction. The house was to be mine, the tunnel my passageway, and I would forget my longing for a courtyard. And yet, because I had learnt through the up-and-down years neither to be too convicted in my faith nor have undue faith in conviction, I occupied the days of waiting by another visit to Katápola.

It might as well have been another island. The two-way journey took two and a half days, and once there, so sure I felt again about Aiyiáli, I inquired about no houses or anything but how I could get back. Reconsideration would not help me when I knew where I was going, and since I knew that I must somehow find the means.

Only the warmth of a summer night refuted my sleepy muleback whim as I came up again, Langátha is a glacier. The source rose at the summit, in the *platía*, and slowly flowed into the gorge, edging into rifts, receding around rocks, spreading down the one flank exposed towards the winter river and the plain beneath, once — where the water churned — rising up to an acropolis, and as all solidified and stood in place eking into a final trickle to meet its people coming from the sea.

A fine thought that might be, but where was I to live? The acting landlord of the tunnel house found me in the *platía*. 'My brother says twenty thousand drachmas, and he won't take less.'

'Twenty thousand? But they told me in the spring....'

'They told you, yes, but they were thinking in the past. You could have had this one for half — a quarter — if you had come two years ago. But now we are promised electricity, and a road. Think of it, if you come next year there will be taxis to the bottom of the village. No one wants to sell, they're waiting for a rise in value, or if they do they want the triple price.'

Twenty thousand drachmas is nearly seven hundred dollars, and the house was not yet habitable. 'We will find another,' said Marco, 'you and I,' and various other people made various helpful remarks in as far as a friendly anxiety to cheer is helpfulness, and many advocated patience, which I did not have.

'What are you to eat tonight?' Kyría Mouska said. 'Shall I fry you two eggs?' She was frail and grey and deferential, and though she never used the familiar form when speaking to me I had become familiar as her charge, and the kindness of her features was refined. But still my typewriter was standing in her room cased up with such impatience that the keys were almost working of their own accord, my half-completed typescript was shut up and languishing beside, and I, with a two-month deadline and that love with which a sculptor polishes his finally revealed marble work, fretted uselessly over my wine. Buying or renting were equal to me now.

'Kyría Mouska, how much do I owe you?'

'Well,' she said, 'the eggs cost me three drachmas and the wine four. You haven't eaten any bread to speak of, so that's seven.'

Endearing as the bill might be, I was learning the disadvantage of coming to a place entirely ungeared to tourism. I told her that she should acquire a business head, gave her eight drachmas and appealed, 'What shall I do now?'

'What about that big house over there?' She pointed to a mansion a hundred yards or so towards the cliff. 'Ask for Costa at the bottom of the village early in the morning. He's one of the Roussos family that own it. It won't do, it's too big, but you could look at it.'

Costa was an early riser. I looked for him at six o'clock the following morning and he had gone out 'to the animals' leaving my hope to dangle until after dark. I went down to the beach to give twelve-year-old Irene her first lesson in the alphabet. She came with grapes, told me to pick tomatoes as I pleased, and afterwards her two Athenian aunts, Michali's sisters, called me into their summer house. Each had a daughter in need of English lessons, and though they could offer very little money they would be glad to cook for me. The system was falling into place. I lay in the sea and the three-eyed mountain above this scene of such haphazard commonsense insisted upon adding reassurance. Happiness at unreasonable moments is one of the most important qualities of life. 'The bay,' I thought, 'is beautiful,' and that for the moment was sufficient, and I was pleased that for a space of time I had not been allowed to distract myself with rooflessness or other such interference. I went back to my cottage and there was a fish lunch on my table, with cold vegetable salad and a lemon beside.

Costa, simple-faced, about thirty-five and kindly, arrived at Marco's shop a little before sunset. He took me along a path leading from the *platía* towards the country and opened a gate in the high wall running parallel to the village street from which it was divided by a field. The L-shaped house stood on two sides of a courtyard, green with lemon trees, an apple tree, and shrubs that were trying to be flowering. Crumbling arches shaded the way into the old, now disused storerooms beneath a long, paved balcony to the living-quarters up above.

The flight of steps at one end was overgrown with apple branches, the main way up was broad and lordly, we walked along flagstones around which some mountain greenery, mistaking its environment, had turned the floor into a loosely fitting jigsaw — poor plants, there is little hope for growth along this boulevard. We passed two doors and turned the corner while I tried to remember the importance of being critical. Then Costa unlocked the last door, facing seawards, and I was confronted with the aerial front room.

The floor was wooden, the ceiling wooden, all slightly aged, like a palace that has been — but not for too long — deserted of its king. Greek architecture, if one can generalise, resists the sun, but two sides of this high room were lined with doors and windows looking out on mountains, village, sea. Greek houses are either bare or cluttered; here everything was solid and in proportion to the room, an iron bedstead, tables, chairs, a sideboard, two rare chests of drawers, a heavy mirror crested dustily with floral cupids — all that was not functional — hanging over one, and among each piece was spaciousness in which to walk.

'It's a nice house,' said Costa proudly, 'isn't it? It belonged to the mayor of all Aiyiáli many years ago. This part is the dowry of my sister-in-law, the other is her sister's, but that's been shut up for years. This is the kitchen, and here's another little bedroom....'

'My dressing-room,' I thought, unable now to oust the possessive adjective.

'The well is below,' he went on. 'Yes, it has water all the summer. It's a good house,' he repeated, 'but unfortunately, for you, it is too big.'

It was big, but its size had quartered from the original impression since the house consisted only of the upper floor, and only half of that. And yet the whole enclosed area, outhouses, almond trees and orchards at the back, belonged in practice to the occupant of these three rooms. I said, 'I like it, and this is a good table, steady for a typewriter.'

'But they say you want to buy, and this is not for sale.' He was playing with the key as if anxious to lock up.

'If I moved in here now I might find something else for sale later on.'

'There are no sheets,' he said.

'I have my own.'

'No kitchen equipment.'

'That's small-stuff, I will buy it.'

'But for one person. . . .'

'At any rate,' I urged, 'tell me how much your brother wants a month.'

'Two hundred and fifty drachmas,' he said mournfully, and that, as near as no matter, was three pounds. 'Of course if it were mine I might make it less for you, but my brother says so much or not at all.'

'Costa,' I said, 'I will pay the rent, and why should you worry if the house is large? What difference does it make to you if there is only one person walking from room to room?'

He smiled, he was relenting. 'All right,' he said, and handed me the key. Then in the enthusiasm of having yielded he added, 'It's a good house, all ready, you could sleep here tonight. Why pay Kyría Mouska another ten drachmas for her room?'

Tonight! I wondered if I looked half-witted as I agreed with him. And then he found a lamp, drew water, felt the mattress, and finding it lumpy laid another covering.

I asked, 'When was the house last occupied?'

'A teacher rented it two years ago.'

So all the time there was one house to let in the village that I had chosen, the very house that I had looked for all along, and all this perfection which I had aimed at had existed, and but for Marco's wife I might never have discovered it, for no one had told me because it was 'too big'.

I ran down to collect my luggage while a little light remained, and lighted a candle in the church of Ayia Triádha the next day.

CHAPTER THREE

The Gloved Hand

FEELING self-consciously like a religious on the verge of ecstasy, I uncased my typewriter. One day had been enough for domestic preparation, the house and I were ready, my papers spread over the mayor's old dining-table. I laid the machine beside them, and it did not work. For five years I had been carrying it on the most rickety of journeys, owned it for fifteen, and now for the first time — not a movement could I produce from it — it failed me.

It was early morning. I ran like a mother whose child has been seized by an unknown, possibly fatal, illness, down to the *platía* where a crowd of would-be mechanics immediately surged. Later in the summer Costa, standing in my doorway, said reverently, 'I have seen one of those before, but I have never seen one work,' and I think that the experience of those enthusiasts was much the same. One appeared in his pyjamas with a screwdriver, and together we eagerly worked the faulty carriage so far out of place that after an hour we had contrived to make it difficult to fit obtrudingly into its case. 'It will have to go to Athens now,' they said.

The *tachidhrómos* was leaving in the evening. According to the dictionary he is a postman, but every island has two at least of different callings, the one deliverer of letters, the other errand boy to the capital. Since our *tachidhrómos* left Aiyiáli once a fortnight this was the best moment for calamity.

Calamity? I thought it so at first until I found myself forced into a salutary week of solving all my problem pages before the pleasure became possible of dealing with clean stationery in triplicate. When the place that one was looking for is found all problems are minor and can be overcome; I was living in the mayor's house now. The typewriter came home at last with a four-hundred-drachma bill, and I realised more forcibly than ever that any possession outside island life should be understood from top to bottom by its owner. Apart from the price of carriage to Athens one allows by such a method full scope to the mechanics there to charge what suits their whim. Almost every fortnight I was giving some perverse directions to the *tachidhrómos*, and wished as many times, while we sighed together over the result and he refused his fee, that I had thought more scrupulously beforehand of everything that Amorgós was unlikely to provide.

Those four hundred drachmas came directly from the housing fund, and another two hundred disappeared in the *platía's* grocery on objects which I could pretend were eventually to provision some other house. Love for the mundane things of life possessed me, the everyday necessities, the practical, the choice between two teaspoons or two plates, the stones with which I prop my shutters open, the hammer — the only utensil already in my house — for knocking up the catches and cracking almond shells, and for earthenware bowls in dark glaze with white doodles that are sold for a third of the price of china plates.

Quick and young and pretty, the grocer's wife Ioanna kept her head while I lost mine. 'This,' she would say, 'is cheaper, and in fact it's better,' or, 'you don't want to spend twenty drachmas on a wine jar; take this now and return it when you leave.' To such practical people as the inhabitants of Langátha it was commonsense, when two days later an English couple walked into the village and made a rare request for lodging, to tell them, 'Wait for your compatriot, she usually comes up at sunset.' And it was fortunate that when I arrived in the *platía* I immediately liked Peter and Margot who were waiting for me in accordance with the instructions of the village, since I could hardly have gone into revolt.

'But what shall I do with them?' I asked Kyría Mouska. 'The man has a sleeping bag, but the woman . . . ?'

She said, 'I can lend you a camp bed and sheets. They are foreigners, it is fitting that you should take them in, you have the room. But if they stay then they should pay you, that is right since you pay rent.'

Margot stayed with me for the best part of a week while Peter performed the mad Englishman around the island, losing weight on steep paths at the time of day when everyone else avoids them, and when he returned to us, rather red and shiny, the village murmured approbation at the episode. We asked Vangelió at the central *magazí* if she could provide aubergine and garlic sauce that evening, but, 'Perhaps you should go to Kyría Mouska,' she demurred, 'we mustn't hurt her feelings.'

The foreigners were due to me, and we to Kyría Mouska. I wondered for an anxious moment whether the summer would appoint me permanent hostess to aliens, but after all if foreigners did make a regular appearance in the village the inhabitants would all have rooms to let and know something of the sense of competition.

These two left, my typewriter came back, and I felt that I had been settled in Langátha from the beginning of all time, and did not know about the passing of the days among the natural routine. 'I hear you want to buy a house.' Thus I was intercepted once on my way home. To buy? Oh no. Langátha has been promised electricity, Langátha has been promised asphalt, can I afford to buy a house? I have no time to look at one, no inclination, no house is better than the mayor's. I am embezzling my brother's dollars — Henry, I am embezzling your dollars and I am far too happy to apologise. The cobbler plays his violin in the *platía* and I dance along my balcony; my own stones are good enough to stamp on — I am an aristocrat, I am a mayor myself. Hi there stars and circumstances! Listen to the music, I pulled a fast one unintentionally and no one who is happy has the right to be ashamed.

Life in the right place takes the right action of its own accord. Soon Yorgo from the bottom of the village, fourteen years old and shy but nicely mannered, was arriving at my house four days a week at nine or ten for English lessons, and another of those accidental arrangements which one discovers functioning was part of the routine. Yorgo's mother is a dressmaker, a hard-working woman with charm and sense who keeps her three boys in new suits for festivals, while the father, tender of the family fields and animals, waives the right of learning and of elegance to them and makes up with simple-hearted smiles. They paid me even less than the two girls on the beach and I reaped the benefit. Yorgo's mother washed my dresses, Yorgo's mother solved my problems and mended my neglected clothes, she sent the boy with a cake or grapes to English lessons, and when the hens stopped laying, as they are inclined to do in summer, Yorgo's mother deprived her children of the rare egg and sent that too, so that I had to pretend to have another source.

Yorgo's mother in the village, Sophia's mother on the beach, became pillars which I had not looked for, which I could not have done without. Sophia, Irene's cousin, at eleven was my quickest student, she covered a year's English course in those two months, and since her mother found it unpractical to cook at midday and leave out one neighbouring head I received my daily meal according to the Greek sense of what an appetite should be. There always was something to be carried up and doctored with more herbs and wine at night, and gradually my heavy basket grew in weight up that long hill as laden donkeys passed, fig pickers paused at work, and Yorgo's mother added to it at the top. Where everyone lives off his fields and is largely self-providing there are no greengrocers, and where shops are lacking everything is free. I could never take a step without a basket, or how could I have coped with offerings? A hundred dollars on Amorgós is wealth.

Even my wine flagon was refilled less often than at any other time in Greece. Working alone in the evenings and never wanting to go out, I found that my own walls contained me and were temperate. What has Aiyiáli done, I wondered, to create this spotless character to whom I have just been introduced? Such is the power of the village, I am hardly responsible. When I settled first on Mykonos in its earlier days of tourism I began life by making every possible mistake. Could it be done, I wondered, to enter another island and be someone else? It can. Langátha had decided to respect its foreigner, so I could not make mistakes, I was respectable.

I could not, that is, make moral mistakes, or social ones, but while all that went well became blurred in the business of existence I do remember making a romantic mistake over a bag of wool. When in life can one come to the point of always being right? I think — I hope — that it would be very dull. It did seem to me that, since I had lost my heavy sheep-back sweater bought on Mykonos from Vienoula, it would be a beautiful and economical idea to have a new one made on Amorgós. Sheep there are, the women spin, and half the island's woollen clothes are home-produced. 'Welcome . . . Good evening . . .' the figures sitting through the nightly greetings, gathered in tiers up the long curving stair, are twirling distaffs in their fingers, turning into skein the fluffy bunches of their carded wool towards a vest or sweater for their sons. Surely, I thought, it would be an act of some benevolence to give a taste of foreign trade.

I began enquiries with Yorgo's mother and was passed from hand to hand until some woman insisted on wasting half an hour of her morning to take me to some hag who might, she said, have wool, but might also be inclined to cheat were I alone. Wool off a sheep's back is not very prepossessing. We haggled darkly in her hovel among a density of obscure objects, cats and all the grime and smell attached which the summer months had failed to dry out. Holding her scales in what air there was, the woman balanced two oily bundles on it and pronounced the amount two *okas*, forty drachmas' worth. 'It's good wool,' said our intermediary, and I was charmed to be going through sweater-making the natural if unsalubrious way. What next? What happens to it now? My friend looked worried. 'It needs washing, I would do it, but. . . .'

I carried it to the *platía* and appealed to Kyría Mouska. She would wash it. Of course I could depend on her. She lit a fire in her kitchen and gave it its first wash with a series of ungrudging frowns. It was a cold day, I remember, suddenly we had been given a foretaste of the winter, and when the wool was ready for the rinsing we spent a shivering half-hour in the garden lugging water from the well and sacrificing Kyría Mouska's slippers. 'It's very short,' she said, pulling the tufts apart. 'There is one good sheep and one bad sheep here.' I hoped that if we mixed them up the bad sheep might be lost among the good.

We spread the heavy mass out on my balcony to dry, and then it rained and Kyría Mouska refused payment however much I urged her, for she seemed to think that it would be excessively unfortunate to have to pay for what already called for sympathy. However I had my wool, it dried, a breeze came up and every hour or so I collected strands hanging tastefully among the lemon trees. I pulled out the flecks of all those bits and pieces that a sheep collects around the mountains in its life, supposed that it was less uncomfortable for a beast than for a person to go without shampoo, and looked forward to transferring it to my own back.

But who would spin it for me? Which of those multitudinous distaffed women should I patronise? The question quickly changed direction, which would patronise me? Kyría Mouska was spinning her own wool for her family, and so was every other woman in the village. Who has time on her hands in this community? Not one single woman. This was my basic error in the enterprise, I did not know how to spin.

'How's the wool?' my neighbours called as if to say, 'How's the baby?' and every day the question left me increasingly embarrassed. One girl in the country half promised to knit me a sweater once the wool was spun, and Kyría Mouska said that I should have it sent to Naxos to be done by machine. I recoiled at this outrageous suggestion, deafened myself to her words that this would be not only quicker but less costly, and stuffed the wool into a polythene bag with a strong impression that one of the initial *okas* must have been the weight of oil and dirt. Two sheep's backs, one would think, would cover one of mine — I combed the lemon trees for fragments — but I was beginning to lose faith.

Eventually I carried it — sheepishly one might say — to Mykonos where my old friend Stavroula, wife of Petinos on Platí Yialó, regarded it with misgiving and me with some reproach. 'This is no good, Carolina, it's all broken up, look, this is how we spin.' She tugged at a lump of almost live wool entirely undoctored and turned it like a magician into a long even skein.

'On Amorgós,' I nearly said, 'they card the wool,' but I refrained. I could hardly tell a woman of the island which is rich from tourist weaving how to learn her trade from Amorgós. Anyway I could not go on carrying this bag, like Christian's burden, on my back, so when I went to Athens and later on to England I left it there. I came back in the spring to be presented with four balls of wool which Stavroula's daughter-in-law, Photiní, had spun. 'But it's very fine,' she said, 'it will have to be used double. The work was difficult.'

I sold the wool to Vienoula for a hundred drachmas and gave half to Photiní. So I broke even as far as the expenses went, and in the meantime had bought an English lambswool sweater. And the moral of that is that one should touch nothing on Aegean islands that one does not understand. Life is very simple once that truth is grasped.

The first subject to master, if one wants communication with the outer world, is the boat system, and that on Amorgós is difficult. During the summer one of the Dodecanese boats is required by the government to make a stop here, ten hours from Piraeus direct and twice a week, so that if on one's first introduction to the island one happens to coincide with the right day one thinks it among the most conveniently accessible of the Cyclades. But the summer timetable begins one week without announcement, or makes an announcement and does something else; Athens claims that one boat stops at Katápola, the other at Aiyiáli, but does not like to commit itself to which does which. Then both boats stop at both ports, sometimes at Aiyiáli first, sometimes at Katápola, and then they change their days; however, they do come. Besides this there is the pottering boat which runs once a week in summer, and, out of season — when it has the not much sought-after monopoly — twice a month. One of the most elderly and most dishevelled, this makes a long circle in opposite directions on alternate weeks among half the Cyclades, usually, except in summer, as far as Santorini so that one never knows at what time it will arrive, and usually, but not always, stopping at both ports.

The shipping agent of Aiyiáli is a grocer in Langátha, and the most reliable prediction is his summer saying, 'We have a regular timetable now, only it may change days.' It is not always convenient that the shipping agent lives half an hour's mule-ride from the harbour, it is not always convenient that if you are waiting for a boat to go in one direction it may turn out to be going in the other, but it is certain that if a boat is coming determinedly from the direction in which you want to go there is no use in protest or in argument. This is especially true of the caïque which links Katápola and Aiyiáli with Naxos and its dependent islands 'regularly'. But the most important thing to be learnt about the system is that if a boat is going somewhere, then a journey, to wherever that boat is going, can be made.

Insularity is quick to make its impact, and after a few days the coming and going of boats means nothing more than spectacle, a piece of conversation, 'How punctually the *Polikos* came in this morning!' or, 'How late!' — 'Did anyone come off the *Marylena?*' — 'Was it held up by storm?' Oh, we are no longer interested in journeys, but we must know that twice a week there is a party at the harbour in wineful waiting for the eleven o'clock boat, when the muleteers' *magazí* — or so I call the fishiest — is sizzling, and every light is on. Dusty figures are converging from Thollária, Langátha, Potamós, their suppers in little billy-cans, ordering plates, forks, salt and a steady flow from the retsina barrel. Around the corner, arched along the waterfront, Kyría María's *magazí* draws her twice-weekly maximum of crowded customers, and she, turning whom she does not want away severely, places with a smile a piece of fish or saucerful of olives beside another who has no food 'for his wine'. Ioanna, her beautiful, deaf daughter, turns up the record player in boat-night glee, converses wildly with the proficient people of Aiyiáli, and revels in a dance. Now the boat hoots, the policemen look important, and the muleteers gulp down their last glass.

This should be known; know too that on another evening the harbour will be asleep by nine o'clock, that midday depends on its surrounding nights, that if a midnight boat comes in at dawn Kyría Maria's siesta must begin at twelve o'clock. 'Coming in at this time!' she ejaculated scornfully when I arrived at one, while often at a later hour, when she feels like complying to the request for wine, she charged two drachmas for a tumblerful, a piece of bread and whatever else she feels like offering from the pot.

The boat hoots, and somewhere there may be letters for us, or perhaps, as is the chief rule of off-season months, they have gone to Naxos first. Thence, about twice a week depending on the weather, they are taken by caïque to Katápola and the *Chora*, thence over the mountain on muleback with Vangeli the far-travelling postman, rested in Potamós on the way down to the harbour and now, if impatient for communication, we can catch him before his final ride around Langátha and Thollária. He is arriving, he is drawing out his little bugle, 'Come! Listen to what news is out of date!'

Since ten days is a good rate for a letter, either from another island or from England by airmail, I soon realised that communications of any urgency must be made by telephone or cable, and only with great patience if by telephone, since one person on the whole island can have a conversation at one time. A little desk in the corner of Miki's *cafenion* at the harbour functions as telegraph and post office, though stamps are not always to be had and if they are we weigh our letters in our hands and sometimes stick on an extra drachma's worth for certainty. Each village has its office of this kind.

Miki, a little grey old man with gentle lines of worry spread about his kindly but defensive face, wields his receiver as if concentrating, until the early evening when we shut down to the world, on warding off the evil eye. I did not help. I had a perverse habit of trying to send telegrams in English, which he did his best to cure and wisely, for when I received the same I had to go through a long decoding process before understanding the result. 'This *omega*,' I would say then, 'should be like this,' and 'demonstrate a 'W', but it was I, not he, that needed to apologise. 'Why should I know?' he would ask me, 'I don't know your alphabet.' And why should he?

'Kyría Carolina!' An infant messenger charged into my midday lesson with Sophia. 'Miki wants you, you have a telegram.' I answered that I was expecting it, I knew the contents roughly and would collect it in the afternoon. This was unkindness and I repented when I came in slowly towards six. Miki was sitting on his doorstep like a lost mariner searching for a sight of land. 'Praise God!' he exclaimed in confusion between crossing himself and seizing the red-hot piece of paper from his pocket, and thrust it — 'Can you read it?' — at my hand.

It was a bleak day in Miki's summer when I had to send a telegram to England, and one of indetermination in my own. The question had arisen of whether or not I would go back for the winter and I could not make up my mind. Finally, I made out a cable saying 'yes', writing the letters in clearest capitals, and asked him to send it at nine o'clock the next morning, which gave me time to change my mind and ring him from Langátha. Even though I repeated my instructions several times I knew I was not doing well. 'Send it unless I ring,' and yet without doubt I must ring him anyway. The next morning the village was engrossed in heatwave and I in the final stages of my book. Our telephone office was at the bottom of the village, and I was feverish. 'I will go now,' I thought and inserted a new page in my typewriter. 'Well,' I thought, 'I did tell him to send the cable if I don't ring...' and I did not go.

I stayed all day in Langátha and the next morning walked down to the harbour. 'Did you send the telegram, Miki?'

'But, Carolina, you didn't ring.'

I sat down worried, for now it would be late, and he sat down worried too, and we looked at each other like creatures allied in misfortune for which neither was responsible, 'After all,' we said, 'it hasn't gone so what's the use ... ?' He took up the receiver to get to work on this outlandish chore, and in the evening when I passed again informed me that his part had been performed. 'Haven't we got some fish?' he asked his wife. 'Give some to Carolina,' and she picked out six small eel-like serpents from a bucket; they made delicious soup.

I much prefer to suit than being suited, to be the glove that fits a hand, not the hand that requires fitting, for only then does one belong to a landscape, no more obtrusive than a rock, while that landscape takes on a friendlier appearance because one is part of it. The philosophy of Aiyiáli towards foreigners is even extended to our one hotel, which, standing on the waterfront, is clean with lovely views, water in all the bedrooms, and good cooking of food brought in from Naxos served by quiet and attentive girls in uniform. Full *pension* is the only price, and an air of regimentation rules among the residents. How else could the proprietor calculate on how much food to cook, and when, or — if there were a choice of menu — how much of what kind? But the proprietor of our hotel does not accept as problematic what must surely be a widespread catering problem. At one o'clock and nine a bell is rung, and all participants must be at hand to eat what they are given, for the late arrival is too late to eat at all.

The few hotel guests came and went and made small impact. Athenian relations, island-born, came in for the summer holiday, and for a fortnight over the feast of the Virgin Mary Stephanáki the cobbler, 'little Stephan', spent more time with his violin than with his shoes. Parties were held nightly, and during one the chilling moment recurred when my typewriter broke down, and in the middle of a flight of inspiration I burst in to have it healed on the floor beneath the pounding feet of the *calamatianó*. That was a farewell party, what had happened to the summer? It had a beginning and an end, but it did not have a middle, only a timeless piece of existence in between. The Athenian boys brought pop music and a travelling company the shadow play of Karajoz, and the islanders partook or not of their enjoyment and continued with their work, and so did I.

Gentle in manner, masterful in action, Costa, one of the best dancers in the village, allowed no late night to upset his risingtime. Hastily between his other works he would come in to see that all was well, to lay down rat poison or pick his absent brother's fruit, and coming upstairs with a heap of grapes or figs allow a short time for an ouzo or a coffee while he admired the mystery of touch typing, questioned me about the moon and answered my own questioning about the house.

'It was more beautiful,' he said, 'before the earthquake. The house trembled — that corner fell right off and the family could not afford to have it well repaired.' Certainly the ceiling is not quite up to mayoral standard; the windows, shutters, doors need greatest tenderness in opening and shutting, and the door which overlooks the village opens — filling me with horror — on to a balcony which is not there. Only three decaying beams jut out to remind the occupants of how it had been before the earthquake flung it off, forcing one to look up at the massive wall of rock behind and mutter a prayer to the infernal gods. 'All the people living up there,' Costa said, 'were very nervous. That was 1957. The sea went back one hundred metres and Nikouriá' — the islet which stands out to sea between Aiyiáli and Katápola — 'burnt for three days. No one was killed. No one was even hurt. Carolina, have you eaten any almonds yet?'

'I collect the ones that fall.' High summer was passing and I remember conversations in connection with specific days.

'Do that,' he said, 'for otherwise the rats will get them, and I shall have no time except to pick the trees. How hot it is today! The heat is bad for work.'

The air was heavy and the leaves unmoving. A bikini on the shaded garden wall was hot, and the wind which came up in the afternoon hot too, and the almonds rattled down. The night was for lying naked beneath an open window in the southern gale, and some time in the early hours for shivering awake. 'It will rain,' they said, and we put on winter sweaters. 'The rain is good.'

To know the time of leaving can be as difficult as to know where one's own place is or when to come. I was the last of summer visitors, and the time had come to forget a preference for the term 'inhabitant'. Two months on Amorgós was not long, but the right amount. Now Michali's family came down less often to their seaside orchards, and sometimes Irene did not arrive at all, or rode down especially to have a lesson and got a headache on the way, and the English book to which she had progressed began to lead us farther from the island. 'Mary goes to school by car. Car, Irene, *to aphtokínito.*'

She wrote it down, paused, and made the confidence, 'I once saw one of those. I haven't been in one, but we went to Katápola when I was six, and I saw.'

So, 'Mary goes to school by car and John goes to school by bus. Bus, *to leophorío*,' and she wrote it down. Then she frowned and asked me, 'What do you have in a *leophorío*? People?'

A bus is like a boat. It has regular stops — more regular than boats — where passengers get off and on with tickets according to the route. Now that I come to think of it, no one could have gone to school by bicycle or I would have remembered that more tricky definition. Meanwhile *pagotó*, ice cream, is like creamy milk, frozen yet not hard, sometimes with egg in it, sweet with various flavours such as fruit or chocolate. I did not think it sounded very nice, and what, anyway, is cream? Irene sighed, 'Shall I fry you two eggs?' she said. 'We are very busy in the village and I don't want to be back late.'

Sophia's mother had departed with her family to Athens. I scrubbed around the orchard for the last, dwindling tomatoes and otherwise began a diet of potatoes, almonds and dried beans. Irene had learnt an alphabet as mysterious as buses, and now her enthusiasm had to take a rest. She said, 'I'm leaving in a week or so. I'm going to stay with my cousins in Athens and go to grammar school.'

Irene! My God!

'So I'm very busy getting ready. Do you have some grapes? I'll bring you more.'

She seemed to be more calm about the matter than I could myself, and a week afterwards had left. Well, she would be shattered for a short time and take it in her stride. I saw her on the last day standing robustly among the fading vines, and felt a pang as I called after her, 'Don't forget to eat ice cream.'

My back ached from typing and re-typing, for the book had to be completed here and I not leave too late. I went to sleep at night in the middle of a sentence and woke almost before the sun to finish it. Hasty dances on the balcony grew comma length, the ribbon faded, the last page I had was used, and so I stopped.

I spent the evening before I left at Marco's *magazí*. Autumn hours rested on the village while he played bouzouki records and every other light went out. Here for the first time I danced before spectators. I danced my thanks and triumph for Marco and Kyría Mouska among their tables and out on to the dark *platía* floor.

'Did I go mad?' I asked, the next day.

'No, you did well,' they said.

I ordered a mule for nine o'clock and under-estimated the time required to clip together twenty-five chapters and a preface in triplicate with all the edges straight. Dark fell, I was still at work, and Costa came in to help shut up the house.

'Did you write all these pages?' He sat down, half wise, half at sea. 'Yes, but will they find a publisher?'

He looked closely, paused and said, 'I don't understand a single word, but I like it, I would have it. What is it called?'

'*I Trellí Rodhiá*, The Mad Pomegranate Tree. It's from one of your own poets.'

'A strange name,' he said. 'Perhaps you mean *The Mad Evening?*'

'No, not *vradhiá — rodhiá.*' We laughed away our perplexity, and while Costa made a mental inventory of all my kitchen equipment, to be guarded with Amorgot sense of value for the following year, it occurred to me that I had better not reclaim it until that madness had been justified.

I changed into slacks to become a tourist for the boat. Would it be a night, I wondered, when Aiyiáli pretends that it has no young men or motor engines and Miki, tired already from making telephone calls and coffee, rows us to the steamer?

'Are you sorry to leave, Carolina?' Everybody asked the same.

Neither sorry nor happy, for everything is right.

The muleteer, Irene's uncle, had arrived, and we piled my luggage out of doors. 'Goodbye, house.' Costa put out his hand and gave me one pat on the head. It was the equivalent of first-night rape on Mykonos.

CHAPTER FOUR

The Goat's Teeth

HALF of adaptability is a virtue, which ought to be ranked among the seven, ousting prudence, hope or even temperance, any of which may be centred on oneself. All virtues could be concentrated under the one title of philanthropy, which I take literally as 'love of man' rather than sending intermittent cheques to orphanages. It is really the only one that matters, and to be adaptable, which means to live in tune with other people, comes nearer to it than most. This gift for the non-philanthropist is as difficult as the recognition of a certain key in the ringing of a doorbell for the non-musical, but is nevertheless of paramount importance in this overcrowded world.

But I repeat that only half of adaptability is a virtue, for if everyone spent his whole existence tuning in to others no one would know what the tune is, and life becomes a piano with a cat dancing on the keys. Half of oneself should be oneself.

I had been living too long in other people's houses, in England, Turkey, Italy and Greece, almost consecutively from the time that I left Amorgós in 1966 until Easter 1968. I had not claimed the key from Costa in the intervening summer, I had not claimed the stove and saucepans, or the pile of scribbling-paper for the first draft of some new book. I had neither been back nor heard one word of news. One's own place, the place where one is self-possessed, is not for casual treatment, and if one's head is temporarily knocked off balance it is better to be somewhere else. Illness saved me from returning to Langátha with my mind at the wrong angle, and I in a gutless way was relieved to have had the decision made for me.

Now, the next year, now that I was ready, with the book that I had finished there in proof and my head clear for a new one, the island was my aim again. But how could I be sure in Athens that the mayor's house of Langátha was still standing, that Costa would keep it for me, that there was still no electricity, no road, and the complications and expense which both would bring? A letter would be useless. To be sure of spending the summer in that house I must go there in the spring. This was the season of the pottering boat alone, running once a fortnight and — on the day when I was free to go — running in the wrong direction round its circle. It remained the only way in which I could achieve my mission, so I boarded it on the early date of 15 April.

The *Myrtidiótissa* is one of those boats long since rejected from the English Channel crossing, and in the gale which blew up as soon as we passed Cape Sunion I was too occupied being frightened to be sick. Not so the four other occupants of my little cabin, who in their last gasp of humour retching from exhausted stomachs laughed that among their own islands their nurse should be a foreigner. After an unpleasant night we reached Pholégandros, and the last of these half-dying women — thank God, I was going to be rid of every one of them — began to stagger up while I reported how we were drawing in, could see the figures on the quayside, see the rowing-boats, see — oh, no, no thanks to God at all — that we were drawing out again.

My companion, whom I would call a wraith had she not been so portly, made many references to God as well while we retreated from the unprotected harbour. Was she to be carried on to Santorini, thence to return to her island by caïque? I shuddered for her, but her plight was not so harsh. She had only to wait for the boat to circumnavigate the island to the more sheltered bay towards the south, sway down the gangway into a rowing-boat which heaved on swell up to a jetty on to which she must be hauled, there steadied for a moment, and put on to a mule to climb an hour's trek of blasted mountainside to reach her village and her home. After a wait of several hours I followed her ashore, and admired the boatman's skill in landing those of us who yearned for *terra firma* without breaking up his boat against the landing-stage. The *Myrtidiótissa* was sticking to its cliff.

'Don't go far,' the captain said. 'If the wind drops and we can leave we'll hoot for you.''

After a short consideration of his words I persuaded two young Americans to take the hour's walk with me to the *Chora*.

If anything were ever certain about boats, the *Myrtidiótissa* was going to shelter in this harbour overnight, but having gone to some lengths to say that it never is I cannot say that I was justified. However, I do believe that optimism in gloomy moments, madness in what seems unmitigated misery and various other obstinate qualities of that sort are virtues if not carried to excess. They are the discoverers — or creators, if there is none ready-made — of that one per cent redeeming feature which will change places with all the other ninety-nine in retrospect. I was thoroughly pleased now that we were having such a ghastly journey, for it enabled me to see the *Chora* of Pholégandros, a village to which from time to time I had considered making a special expedition. It stood up there above us within walking distance to be thrown in gratis and its site and architecture deserved the snatching of an opportunity. So I flouted the captain of the *Myrtidiótissa* and was satisfied, for this was what I would have to keep with me.

The captain treated his passengers badly that night, making up sleep — the best occupation for a rough sea — in harbour, and deciding in the morning that the wind had dropped. As the journey was rougher than before, as it seemed even less likely that the boat, whose one quality in these conditions was valiance, could hold all her joints together for much longer, I presume that he had not the provisions for a seige, or else was considering his company's purse strings.

In the late afternoon we arrived at Katápola, and I went out on deck to see, though not the harbour, the island on whose account I was undergoing this experience. 'Aren't you for Amorgós?' a steward asked me. 'Here you are.'

'But I'm going to Aiyiáli.'

'We don't stop there this time.'

In the face of this announcement, that the journey which had taken two days and four hours was not even delivering me at my destination, annoyance was quickly outweighed by relief. I was to disembark.

Accidents are more often fortunate than not. I like the *Chora*, I like the *magazí* which receives me once or twice a year to strengthen me for or revive me from the mountain. I like to make a stop at the monastery, to light a candle in honour of its rich Byzantine icons, to chat over a liqueur or coffee with whichever monk is standing on reception, to ascertain that the sister of one is my neighbour in Langátha, to hear what foreigners are buying land in these parts, and while saying 'how nice' to all keep to myself my higher estimation of Aiyiáli. Not even my suitcase was a problem, for I had hit on the evening before the postman's ride, so I delivered all my possessions to him in the morning and free of weight of mind or luggage set out in cool but sunny weather for the way with which I had become familiar.

Thus my comic island area imposed on me the most romantic method of re-entry, though the only one practical before the end of April, to stroll in from the *Chora* like a casual pedestrian. 'How clever of you,' people say when I explain how I am established in Langátha, but I answer, 'Nonsense, these things happen, they do not need cleverness so much as patience.' But when they say, 'How lucky you are,' I think of all the obstacles and hazards around Aiyiáli and take the other point of view. Lucky? I am not different from you, I made my life here and you could have done the same if that had been your choice. My dear island, I thought as I bruised my ankle, how I work at you.

Only half of adaptability, as I said, is virtue; more of it than that is the worker of indecision and doubt. When I rounded the corner at which I had stood with Yanni four years earlier, where the long way down to Aiyiáli reveals itself below, I was struck again with one of those flashes of clarity without which, once in a while, life is meaningless. It is a knowledge of being, outside any purpose, accompanied by a crazy happiness which for a moment separates one from the world so that one knows — for hermits are of little use to anyone — how better to re-enter it again. I am glad that I am an earthly being, if not earthy, or I should fall into very deep water here. As it is I know no more than this: oneself is oneself and the world would be far less of a hotch potch if every individual realised it once a year.

I thought, if I fall and sprain my ankle the postman will pass by, and if I sprain my ankle off the track sooner or later he will put two and two together and come and find me, and the knowledge was comforting, but it was comforting as well to know that nobody was expecting me at any place or time, or knew, or was particularly interested, where I was. But I would write a book. When I came back in the summer I would write.

Now that I was here again it seemed so obvious that everything would be basically the same and the house, unoccupied, ready for me again, that no question remained but how to leave. The president was preparing to open a real restaurant and a house of rooms to let beside his quayside grocery, Marco had closed his *magazí*, and that was the sum of Aiyiáli's eighteen-month developments. Costa promised, 'Of course I will keep the house for you. Since I say so now, even if someone wants it for a year I shall not have the right to rent it to anybody else.'

That was that. I began enquiring about boats. Sooner or later, according to the weather, there must be a caïque to Naxos. The wind, to my relief, had dropped, so also had the clouds, they festooned themselves around us in the village and when I climbed into the bed to let above Vangelió's shop in the *platía* of Langátha I got out again to screw myself into the short length of my coat, trying to ward off the sensation of lying among slightly molten ice.

For three days I walked incessantly for warmth, to Thollária, Potamós, and in the mountains beyond the lonely church of the Panayía — the Virgin Mary — where we hold our summer festival, exercise which added to the continual necessity of changing clothes. From Friday to Monday I worked through a suitcaseful, never able to wear one garment for a second time. It did not rain but everything was damp, a matchbox would disintegrate after a few hour's use.

The islanders wear their clothes as the sheep wear their wool, and do not know how great is the discomfort, or, being born with it, that the feeling around the woollen skin is such. But they demand the right to know it when they ask for tourism and progress, and we who are pickers and choosers of our seasons must give them precedence, we must not sacrifice them to being picturesque.

A damp April has all the sordidness of winter; I felt bitterly unwashed. This must always be my summer island, I knew that. And even the summer for the islanders is not a time for swimming but a season when the fields are hot. How can we who admire but do not want to share their stamina deny them the roads and electricity they want?

People of Langátha, when you speak of expecting these developments, and when the foreigners who have visited your village writhe in their distress to hear it, I, who side with them emotionally, will take your part. But do you realise what you are asking for? Your village will not become more beautiful but less so, and the chances are that you will be no happier.

So my mind worked, and then I told myself that I did not come to teach, I came to learn.

I climbed down the gorge below Langátha where the deserted village Stroumbo stands, and looked into the church of Ayios Nikoloas, the only building still preserved. Inside the tiny chapel in the courtyard I found a heap of human bones and skulls. 'Why are these here?' I asked on my return, for usually the bones, once disinterred, are carefully reburied in the church.

Another question was all the answer that I got. 'Did you see the skull of a man a hundred years old with all his teeth intact?'

No, I had not identified a centenarian's teeth.

The young farmer whom I was talking to had been born there, and married there ten years ago, though the houses are so irrevocably crumbled that I had thought them more likely to be contemporary with his grandfather. How significant this seemed. In ten years Stroumbo has turned from a village to a bone more decayed than any of its centenarians, and if a man should live so long up here I doubt if he would die with all his teeth intact.

Every evening, once the retsina had removed the day's chill from the marrow, some delight of conversation was sure to be another warming influence. The villagers were all impressed that that mysterious bout of writing, which had occupied so many weeks, so many pages, was about to turn into a book in a bookshop, though how it had taken so long, and how it had not made me rich, they could not understand. So they set about deciding on the subject of the next one, a matter for which I felt whole-hearted gratitude since I was not sure myself. Conviction may have fallen to me on the way in from the *Chora*, but that was only two days earlier and there was more than minor detail to fill in.

The policeman in particular, a native of Corfu who has lived in Langátha for several years and is happy to continue doing so, took the matter seriously in hand, pacing with contorted face around the *magazí* to bring a store of 'Interesting Facts about Amorgós' to mind.

'For instance, there is this ancient site . . . that stone. . . . For instance, the church of Ayia Triádha, the old citadel. . . . For instance, yes, there is a certain plant on the island which exists nowhere else. You will write about that in your book.'

'What does it look like? What is it called?'

'No one has seen it, nobody knows.'

'But then — ?' Was I stupid not to understand?

'We know,' he said, 'because it makes the goats' teeth gold.'

Everyone was listening with enjoyment, as people do to stories that they know. 'It's true!' an old man shouted. 'I can show you,' and he bolted out.

'Yes,' said the policeman, 'a plant that is unique. And then, let me see. . . .'

But the plant sufficed, and now the old man was running in again with a quarter of a goat's jaw in his hand. What a dental day it had become. 'Look! And many others are more gold than this. Here, keep it,' and he put it in my own.

I treasure my goat's teeth, for they are the substance of my writing, I took them unashamedly as the symbol for what I had seen on the way from Katápola. So thank you my friend, policeman of Langátha, and thank you old man. There is no doubt about the colour of them, but when you ask me, 'Will you put that in your book?' and I say 'Yes', it is not because of the plant that the goat ate or the goat that ate the plant, but because of you.

Let the village dictate. It had dictated a mode of living previously, but then I had not had time to pause and look about. Meanwhile, since Marco has shut up his shop, I am unlikely to make a habit even of an annual dance, but this is not a place for being sentimental about old attachments, life goes on in everyone. '*Kaló ksiméroma*! Good daybreak!' calls Vangelió's mother from her slouching stool when I go home to bed, and even this old woman, a whole face in need of lifting, a kindly and unattractive thing who believes — perhaps because she is herself — that I am a secret addict of early-morning peppermint liqueur, even she has her own moment of enlightenment. Of all the nighttime greetings she at her hidden age has chosen the rare one which looks beyond the night, and I do not care, it is of no importance, if it looks no further than peppermint liqueur.

Three village days had passed, and there were not too many reservations to confidence that the early-morning caïque for Naxos would come in and leave again. I slept the last night at the harbour, smashed my lamp while groping out of bed at half-past four, gathered up in darkness all my possessions that I could find, and gladly boarded the lightly bounding boat, the hard-working forty-footer from Katápola. The decisions of weather and captain had been favourable.

The sky lightened over the sheer outside ridge around Aiyiáli as we set out for Denóusa, Koufounísi and Skinóusa, working down the scale from what is more an island to what is more a rock off Naxos until we came to the little harbour of Iráklia. We were already loaded with islanders, their bundles and their baskets, hens, cheeses, crates and a party of gypsies with a dozen heaps of blankets which they were peddling round the islands and which were put immediately to such general use on deck that their value must have decreased considerably. Everything that one could possibly send from one island to another seemed to be wedged somewhere among us so that even the messages on scraps of paper threatened to be that final straw that breaks the camel's back, and then a late-comer came running up the jetty with a donkey, 'Take this to Naxos too!' and jumped him on.

At two o'clock we landed, after nine hours of skirting the island of our destination. I narrowly escaped a skirmish with the eager donkey and made straight for a taverna to order a large lettuce salad and cancel out the not so much over-full as over-heavy feeling inherited from the diet of Amorgós. Here were tomatoes too. Naxos in fact, so close, was two seasons ahead of the island where for fruit, vegetable and salad in the last four days I had once eaten a plate of cauliflower, probably imported, and once an artichoke risotto made from the wild variety painstakingly gathered from the mountain and painstakingly prepared. A helping of what is in the pot is very cheap, but there are drawbacks at this season.

'We have a good climate,' said the waiter, enjoying my appreciation, 'and good methods. What else will you eat?'

'Another lettuce salad.'

Feeling a little less intense, a little less like a deprived rabbit on the second round, I remembered and began to wonder about the fate of my one companion from Piraeus to Amorgós, a thirty-year-old new Athenian and native of Langátha who had borne the outward journey with a philosophic look of haggardness, and on our arrival, while I slept in the *Chora*, had put on his best city-suit, like every good Greek returning to his village, to ride over the mountain until midnight on a mule. He said, 'That's where I'm going, so I may as well get there,' a sensible remark.

I had met him from time to time in the *platía*, but never sitting, only passing through, nor was he apparent in any *magazí*, and from his quick remarks on greeting I understood that he was not enamoured of his native place. I wondered what his business was, for in pleasure he was certainly not getting his money's worth — or his pain's. 'So we're leaving tomorrow!' he smiled, the day before the caïque left, and it was the first time that he had betrayed the slightest happiness.

But he was not on the caïque. For all his anxiety to leave he had failed to get up in the night, and here was I eating lettuces on Naxos with a choice of boats that afternoon, and there was he marooned two seasons back with no boat to Piraeus for ten days. 'No need to sleep in the harbour,' he had told me cheerfully. 'We'll go together from Langátha in the early morning.' I had disagreed and gone ahead — poor man, he was proved wrong.

I took the boat to Syra, and was astonished half-way through the journey to see my Amorgot friend. Apparently he was a Daedalus. 'Thank the Lord!' he exclaimed, throwing himself down beside me. 'Wasn't that a terrible experience. Look, I have to tighten my belt two holes — two holes! And I'm exhausted. How many kilos have I lost?'

"But how did you get here? You weren't on the caïque.'

'I hired one straight to Naxos.' So that was it, I was put down a pace. When he had spoken to me in the village he had been offering a lift.

'My mother is very ill, she would have died there, I have to take her to Athens to the hospital. Think of it, a whole week of horror, the journey coming and the four days there. I don't know which was worse. I never went out, I sat by her bed, and there was no food to eat. But I don't mind, I did it for my mother, I don't grudge her anything.' A certain radiance shone through his gloomy aspect. 'A mother is the sweetest thing in the world. One wouldn't do it for one's sister, one wouldn't do it for one's wife. But a mother — a mother is worth everything,' and like a lingering invalid exhausted by excessive talking he slumped back into his seat.

It is unusual to meet an islander and find that the common bond of sympathy is the thought of Athens and hot baths. Athens, Makriánni, the Phengári, Julia, I was going to sate myself on them, and every prodigal night would have its purpose, but one which he would repudiate with scorn. My antidote of violent living would be for Amorgós.

My motive for the journey was no more acceptable to him. 'It was for the summer,' I said, and I was thinking that not only for Costa's reassurance, so easy once the words became accessible, also for the walk and for the goat's teeth it had been well made.

'No.' My companion shook his head, a teacher correcting an error in his pupil, 'no. But,' he said, 'you ought to meet my wife and family. Come at Easter, my mother will be out of hospital by then. Come on Easter Day at ten, we'll go to church, and eat, and drink a lot of wine. Have you got a pen? Write down my address.'

He dictated, watched my writing closely, and half-way through corrected me. 'No,' he said, and pondered for a moment, then pointed to a *lamtha*, 'one of those.'

'You write it,' I said.

'I can't, I don't know how.'

He was a nice young man, but in saying no to my opinions he gave me the right to one didactic statement of my own. He should have liked his island or been literate.

Not because of that, but because I was enticed to Euboia, I did not spend Easter with his family. However, I presented myself at his home a few days later and thought, as I put my finger on the doorbell, this is a strange thing to be doing, if only for civility. Our common bond had now become a place to which I was attaching myself because I liked it, while he, from dislike, was breaking real attachment. What perverse and contradictory things human beings are. I want to spend the rest of this summer finding out why I come and why he goes. We are both outsiders, each in our own way.

As was to be expected, his was one of those lugubriously furnished flats in a pre-war block devoid of style or character, too negative if possible to be termed ugly, looking out on nothingness. The worthy son was absent — I wish I knew what work he did — but his wife made coffee for me and we sat politely for a while on hard-backed chairs, she telling me that I had done well to go into the country, the right and proper place for Easter Day.

'Here we did nothing much,' she said, not resentfully but presenting the blank truth. 'We can't go out together because of my mother-in-law, she would have died, you know, if we hadn't brought her here.'

And all the time the old woman sat with her pigtail hanging down, in peasant clothes, sat on her bed with yellow-grey and half-recovered face, grateful and bewildered, admiring, with dim eyes staring out as if looking for Langátha, Aiyiáli, Amorgós.

Part Two

On the Muletrack — 1968

CHAPTER FIVE

The Rhyme and the Reason

THIS year my boat journey coincided with Irene's. She was coming home from grammar school with the two Sophias, her sister and her cousin, for the summer holiday. Sighting each other through the glass doors dividing second class from deck we ran to perform a mime of welcome on each side, in which laughter had to serve for speech. I could see nothing about her that had changed since I left her among the vines two years ago having just explained what buses were. I could see nothing, when we converged to disembark, to be regretted beyond six round loaves of city bread, baked with a hole in the middle for carrying to islands on a string.

'What's this?' I asked. 'Don't we have bread on Amorgós?' I was provocative on purpose because Michali makes such good bread of his own.

'Oh yes,' she said in English, 'but, you know, this is white. I think that you will teach me English now, and perhaps you will teach my sister too.' She paused and added, 'I ate the ice cream. It is very nice.'

I was grateful to her for carrying on the conversation where we had left it. I was impressed by the ease and fluency of her English, which I quote without correction, when only two years ago she did not know the alphabet. So I forgave her the city bread which will soon be disposed of and forgotten, it is no worse than any of our other alien habits that we bring along with us, the remnants of Athens which linger for a day or two and disappear. It is no worse than my wad of paper napkins from the Phengári covered with half-illegible messages which may be of immense importance but are probably of none. All such things must be dealt with and disposed of quickly, then when the house is left uncluttered we are wholly on Amorgós again.

The Phengári is not the taverna-type taverna such as I usually find myself attached to wherever I happen to be in Greece, neither family home nor an ordinary eating-house where working men come in to appease their appetites. It is a grill shop where the inhabitants of Makriánni come to have an evening out. However, the three tables in the kitchen entrance kept 'for our own people' keep also a taverna atmosphere, where any evening superfluities of anguish or high spirits can be readily mopped up with a napkin or a dance, where I can help myself to wine, and where, when words have overflowed the cigarette packets, the paper napkins perform a second use.

'The rhyme and the reason. . . .'
'The swings and the roundabouts. . . .'
'Vassili, give me a napkin.'
'The punished stupidities and the undeserved pleasures. . . .'
Freya says that as an optimist she thinks that if you put them in the balance the undeserved pleasures will win.

'Where is the purpose and where the balance? What is the connection between the swings and the roundabouts?' Everything in May and June had to be justified by something else, and struggled over nightly with verbal mathematics.

The most unpleasant moment of those months involved my car. Perhaps it is natural that a late driver should take pleasure in what most people think a normal situation, and, bitter with self-accusation at a slight mistake, remain in a conscious state of jubilation over the unconscious workings of the hands and feet. I shall always be a beginner at all things because I can never stifle beginner's incredulity at what can be achieved. My arms and legs are elongated and my brain is transmitting messages down into internal places which I cannot understand, which yet respond. Of a thousand monthly miles in Athens and in Attica each one seemed miraculous. And consider what prodigious things are going on each day, for since I cannot differ basically from any other driver, and since I refuse to reduce my own car to the ranks of commonplace I have to raise up all those other millions to join me among the miracles. At any rate it is a more cheerful way than some of dealing with the present traffic problems.

Therefore I was excruciated when I backed at two kilometres an hour into a taxi outside the British Embassy and slightly dented my back mudguard on his unscathed bumper. He was parked in Athenian taxi manner diagonally across a corner, and I almost did it on purpose out of annoyance at his making my turn so intricate. At any rate, I thought, better my own mudguard than his, and would have done well to leave it at that, but I could not. Lugubrious and fatalistic platitudes surged in without resistance, 'There's the first scar.... You're broken in now.... These things go in threes.'

Unnerved at every intersection, stopping more carefully than ever Athenian stopped at all unguarded crossings, looking in more directions, I needed only twenty minutes to allow the words to take effect. Turning into one of those passage streets in Plaka where five kilometres is — or should be — a natural limit because all pedestrians take them for a pavement, I smashed my front right headlamp against the mudguard of another taxi, and in a city of a thousand ramshackle specimens I had chosen one that was brand new.

The crowd was charming. They pushed my car back from the crossroad saying, 'You're trembling too hard to drive a metre now,' brought me water as if I had had a fainting fit and breathed in all my air in the cause of mass attentiveness. Even the taxi driver did not shout at me though everyone was shouting. 'Didn't you look?' I asked him, in my sick unwillingness to make the appearance of a novice at my insurance office.

'Of course I didn't look. I was going straight ahead.' He was an Athenian taxi driver after all.

He arrived at my hotel in the middle of siesta time to verify that I did have insurance, and in his irregular reluctance to lose sight of me drove me and my translation across Athens to my employer's flat. The evening's work there proved as usual an exhausting hilarity for the first two hours and thereafter pure exhaustion, the reading of my English translation back into Greek while my employer followed in the original. 'God in his liberality...' was that how it went? At ten o'clock, after four hours of the exercise, I opened my mouth and could disgorge no sound, while at the same time I discovered that half my concentration had gone into the benumbing of my knees. I walked half-way across Athens to turn them into legs again and left my insurance papers in an ouzo shop.

I hold it as an important rule in life that when one is incurred in unnecessary or uninteresting expense one should add to that one more expense, of flippancy. Since my insurance was third party only, so that a day's work — all that I should have had to put into my purse — was to be lost on replacing my headlamp, I was in honour bound to pay a further penalty at the Phengári. Julia, Julia, make the most of this evening, for this is my new maxim to be adhered to on all scales, let pleasure be the tax on pain.

The human mind is very flexible, and sometimes with a little adjustment or manœuvring one can work out a whole painful incident into the reverse and, if the choice lies in oneself between the pain or pleasure, why not choose to be pleased? Seeing how people behave, for instance, is almost always compensation for a day's annoyance. Again, if I had not been provoking a third accident I could have succeeded in turning the whole day's events into profitable experience, and from there possibly upgraded it to enjoyment. When that cannot be done the tax alleviates.

'Give me a napkin, Vassili.' A cigarette box is not enough tonight. There is support on all sides, sharing in my supper, and perhaps I can confound the picture which perplexingly returns now, of picking figs on Mykonos. In the years when I lived on Platí Yialó in summer, before it became tolerable only in the spring and autumn, fig-picking cancelled out my wine bill to old Petinos. I liked the orchard better than the beach, liked swaying in the branches and, looking up through leaves which dazzled in the sun and wind, discovered that it was indispensable to pick the highest fruit rather than its inferior companions all around. I was mystified, being so familiar with the branches, when one morning I had the sudden conviction, 'I must climb down now or I will fall.' Simultaneously commending and sneering at my caution I walked out of the orchard and without thinking took a short cut by a way that I had never been before, climbing up a ten-foot wall. The top stone slithered in my hand, and wall and I came down together in a bloody heap.

But this is no way to be thinking when handling a lethal instrument among a multitude of other lethal instruments most of which are abominably handled. Oh yes, there are nice white lines along the roads, but the taxi drivers do not know what they mean. Besides, three-quarters of destiny, though we seldom know it, is the result of the connivings of our secret mind. Cassandra was not a prophetess but an intelligent girl who probably today would make a good psychiatrist. Incidents do not go in threes unless we make them do so.

Then come on, flexible human mind, and flex a little, you can surely convince yourself out of any predicament.

I found my answer in New York, in an incident which at the time had seemed symmetrically incomplete, so that I decided now that it had been left there to prove at some later hour of need that life does not need roundness, or else that two half-circles make one whole. I will not attempt a further explanation to such farfetched connivance. If modern life were not so tortuous one would not have to go through such tortuous reasoning, but it seemed to work. I tied up the insurance with a gloom which affected no one but myself and shortly afterwards drove two Americans to the sea. One cannot be temperamental when driving passengers; the shadow became lost, or so I thought.

A couple of days later I had a rendezvous with Jim Price at the corner of Righilis off Vassilias Sophias, and stopped to back before the traffic lights into a one-way street to wait for him. While completing the manœuvre I felt the gentle coming together of my front mudguard with the car — again a new one — on my right. An angry Athenian put his head out of the window and shouted in clear English, 'Young lady, where are your insurance papers?'

Whether or not it is incidental to my point, the scene which I provoked off Vassilias Sophias can certainly be termed a 'typical Greek incident'.

I did not have my insurance papers with me, on which account I received a hearty attack on the obligations of a foreign driver, and so did Jim although he arrived as a passenger a few moments after the accident. I said that I would fetch them, but no, the aggrieved party was afraid that he might lose me. I said that we could go together, but no, that irritated, I should have had them in my car. Every moment of the stalemate became increasingly unpleasant as I thought of the shame with which I must return to my insurance company so few days after my last appearance there. How could I say, 'The most nervous of my friends feels safer in my hands than almost any others in the city, I am a careful driver and said to be a good one, but this was a psychological accident'? A driver has no business to have psychological accidents. I urged that I should pay for the damage privately, but the suggestion was waved aside as futile. After some time of profitless standing about and doing nothing we realised that the Athenian had called for the police.

Jim immediately took a taxi to my hotel to collect my insurance papers himself.

Presently a hot and amiable policeman arrived with a little notebook in which he wrote down various significant facts such as 'father's name — Edgar — *epsilo, ni, taf, gamma, alpha, ro.*' He blinked. It may look odd, but not nearly so odd as William Shakespeare in which the William turns out longer than the Shakespeare. We gradually grew irrelevant. 'After all, it's nothing,' the policeman said, 'Nothing,' echoed the Athenian, 'two or three hundred drachmas at the most. Now you look better. Where did you learn your Greek?' Jim must have been held up in a traffic jam. While we waited for him there was nothing for us to do but chat.

He arrived ten or fifteen minutes later, by which time I was cleaning the car windows ready for the road. The papers had no purpose but to be put in their proper place on the back shelf. The Athenian and policeman had both gone, the former bearing a proof copy of the dust jacket of *The Mad Pomegranate Tree* with promises to advertise it to his friends, while I was versed in the excellence of his daughter's English and encouraged to call at his address. Without the book the outcome might well have been the same, for Jim's delay was leading us in that direction. The book was my opportunity to make the incident more gracious, for I was able to present a copy to 'the man who had been so unpleasant to me' as he called himself, when my six arrived two days before I left for Amorgós. Then I drank whisky in charming company in one of the most exquisite flats in Athens, while my new friend told me that he had kept his mudguard, like a trophy of war, with the dent in.

So in the end I was reprieved from having to look back on any real accident with horror or regret, and that is something about which I deal severely with myself. I do not think that anything once done should be regretted except in certain cases of the misusage, ill-usage or non-usage of someone else, and usually someone who is dead — never in the case of foolishness which leads to trivial annoyances. I know that other exceptions will present themselves, but we would get along much better if that 'if only I hadn't...' could be wiped out of the language. 'If only I had...' could go along with it, because to regret omissions is ridiculous, it is to wish oneself to be another person. Why lament time wasted? All right, it would be delightful to have been more industrious, to have learnt several languages, to have taken all the right opportunities, to have polished oneself in numerous accomplishments. One might as well go further and wish for superhuman gifts and immortality. I and all my wrongnesses are myself, and all people and all their wrongnesses are themselves; the law of balance often cancels out mistakes and we were born with certain weaknesses.

Having finally and delightfully broken from my spell I should have known better as I drove freely about Athens than to go on doing mathematics, but rhymes and reasons and that law of balance continued to be haunting. Where did we get the idea in the first place that good or bad luck has a triple run? It had never bothered me before, but now my mind was busied with that artistic rounding off which is the hallmark of our lives, most of which are better organised than sometimes is supposed. To say that fact is stranger than fiction is ridiculous because fiction has no bounds; however, there are firm bounds to what a novel-reader will accept, and most of the pieces of neat timing and coincidence of which real life is made are too contrived for him.

A friend of mine in Chalkís told me at this time how the year before she had received a telegram announcing her father's sudden death. Given her next month's wages in advance she went straight to the airport terminal to fly home for the funeral, and when she laid all her resources on the counter she found the sum four drachmas short. Then she ransacked her purse again and discovered one four-drachma stamp. I became much attached to this small-scale example of what had been intriguing me, and I am glad to say that when she crowned the pile with the stamp the clerk had the good grace to hand it back.

And what does Aiyiáli have to say of this? Midday sleep has turned the afternoon into a new day, the evening sea has washed off drowsiness and the paved way rises to Langátha through silence only broken by '*Hérete!* Be happy!' from the passing mules and donkeys. This is your moment, philosophy, so get to work.

The figs are ripening, that is how it starts. Then, what a lovely colour Greek brown is, it has absorbed all the forgotten flowers of the spring. The grape harvest will be good this summer, and the olives, which were many and lean last year, are growing few and fat. '*Herete!*' The man rides while the woman walks and a pair of twins sit back to back under blue and white sun hats. Donkey dung, dried in the sun, lies like husks of corn around the stones and smooths off roughnesses; it is a blessing on Greek islands that this unfailing product is of such an unobjectionable and vegetable nature. Now in the village I discover a new snake among the doodles and a fresh flight of verve in flowers, each executed with that careless precision which makes the final loop, neither squashed nor elongated, fit the surrounding petals and the step as if by accident. They fade, they reappear, the exhibition is different every evening, and always it appears that one hand has been responsible from top to bottom, sometimes inspired, sometimes wearying, not that there are white-washers from every house, some more, some less proficient.

Where was I? Where did those serious thoughts disperse themselves along the route? The inhabitants of Langátha, those practical islanders, add a flourish to a more-than-daily chore, sweeping up the donkey dung with doodles.

I should like to put all the politicians of the world, separately, on such an island for a month of every year.

I have been learning greater wisdom from Michali than I ever worked out at the Phengári. This was the result of my effort to avoid a repetition of the one contretemps which took place between us two years ago, but I think it was unnecessary effort. I do not think that I shall be moved around the orchard according to the demands of paying tenants any more. It was not even unreasonable that I should have been that summer, I was only teaching one daughter and as far as I know my little cottage may have been reserved. However, the system led to our only argument: when arriving late at midday I found all my possessions dumped among onions and potatoes in an attic storeroom where there was a bed but blatantly with someone else's sheets.

I took no exception to the potatoes, I rather liked the room, but I suspected infringement on my privacy and was enraged in the heat because at some point in the move my bikini had been lost. On a beach which is the road from the harbour to Thollária, where at any moment a visiting monk—even the abbot from the monastery — might come riding by, a bikini is the very least that can be worn. It is also strategic from time to time in Greece to make a scene, to orate about diplomas and the like, and this I did with vehemence at Michali until the missing article was found and I was sure that I was not to share the new room with anybody else. Once a year is enough on Amorgós, and sometimes, I think now, too much.

I knew how it would be this year when I came down the first day, that Michali would rise up on seeing me to carry beds about and organise his wife and daughters to deal with brooms and water pots, that when I had been swimming I would return to find the spotless, whitewashed box ready for lunch and sleep, with food laid on the table and clean sheets on the bed. They meanwhile were occupying the cottage in which aunts and cousins were shortly due from Athens, where mother was laughing among a a horde of daughters and there seemed to be more curly black heads than ever gathered in one room before.

'Do you know this one?' she asked, pointing to the smallest.

Why yes, of course, I knew that face, but. . . .

'Eighteen months,' smiled mother. Then it was new to me. Woman of Thollária, you have reproduced yourself for the fifth time. It is another girl.

Michali looked on smiling, and I liked him for smiling so without one son among this bunch to raise. How many dowries, I thought, can you afford, and shortly afterwards thought something else, how many daughters shall I be teaching in the next few years? Irene had already made it clear that Sophia, the second sister, was following in her steps.

Rather unwillingly I hunted out Michali to make sure of my position in advance. 'Do you realise that you are asking me for twice the lessons in return for what you gave before?' A mock battle at this stage might save us a real one later on. Michali looked perturbed.

'*Dhespinís* Carolina, do you want me to pay? I can't. If you like, give each of the two girls half the lessons that Irene had before.'

'I certainly don't want money from you,' I told him, beginning to regret what I was saying, 'and I will give them each three hours a week, that's what Irene had and what I choose.'

'Then what do you want?'

Sterling pounds cannot be balanced against pounds in weight, I could not weigh some hours' teaching against tomatoes and a bed. What did I want? Respect. Each must know, and each must be aware that the other knew, something valuable on each side was being done.

'Arrange your lessons,' he said, 'with Irene and Sophia, and teach them when you can. We won't quarrel, I think, this year. You have the house, and whatever else we can give you we will give. Ask for wine, ask for oil, ask for anything you want. If we have it we will give, if we don't have we will say so. *Dhespinís* Carolina, can we make bills?'

He asked the question rhetorically, and we both said 'No'. Then he sent Irene for some cream cheese, and it came with good, brown village bread. The white was finally disposed of days ago.

O logariasmós, the bill, is the calculation, the reckoning, the summing-up that had been teasing me in Athens. Let us make no *logarismó,* said Michali. Wonderful. I like the girls I like my life here. A summer without reckoning — let us have that. One person does not need two houses on a beach, we are not so smallminded in our thinking here.

The undeserved pleasantnesses and the paid stupidities were not to be weighed for a purpose. The thought was uncalculating, and a generous one because it was provoked by parking-fines.

I think that my favourite parable is the one in which the owner of the vineyard pays the early workers their correct wage and then gives the same amount to those who came an hour before sunset. It made me as angry in my schooldays as it made the first arrivals, but no one had reason for complaint.

I have burnt my Phengarí napkins now. I wish that more people than politicians could have the opportunity. I am on the island and my mind is free — I could say vacant because there is room for anything.

Liberation seems strange because we seldom know it, but the mind that is given a holiday throws up its sudden flashes, like dreams that come and go apparently without volition through the night, a theory or a thesis of its own which the islanders would say 'comes on the wind'. I know for instance who are the most important people in my life, do not miss them but am aware of them because they are the only ones who come into my thoughts.

The mind that becomes contorted in the city develops its own sifting process in Aiyiáli.

Strange things happen too in circumstances when one is speaking of no more than everyday affairs and in a language that is not one's own, when speech is easy yet not acrobatic, when one does not complicate oneself by questioning but picks up gratefully whatever may be dropped. Sometimes one understands much more.

I do not think very much on the island, but I listen, I listen to the wind and I listen to the islanders.

'... And my grandmother said, "Tomorrow at eleven o'clock I will die," and the next day at eleven o'clock she died....'

'... My grandfather said much the same, and he gathered the children around him and he said, "I have not been to a lawyer, but this is how it will be, do this and that and that...."'

'Yes, that is the contract between children.' The *cafenion* draws together in approval.

'... And he died, and on the following day his wife died too.'

My own grandfather died after a stroke which laid him unconscious for three days. When the family went through his papers afterwards they found in his engagement book that entries stopped on the date on which the stroke had fallen, but that on the page which marked his deathday there was drawn an exquisite, engraved cross, such as he used to carve in wood.

Rhyme and reason have little business on the muletrack. It appreciates artistry, but does not question it. Don't go pandering, it says, to a society of people who have replaced whooping cough with nervous breakdowns. And how would you solve the death, say, of the world's young geniuses who get knocked down by buses in their prime? What would you balance that against? Oh, there may be promiscuous situations enough when mathematics will be of use again, when obscure ends of life can be tied up to make a reasonable case for isolated horrors, but in the meantime go and paint a doodle on your doorstep and remember that the summer has no reckoning.

CHAPTER SIX

Nature's Priests and Childish Things

I HAVE no poetry with me on the island but what is in my head and Wordsworth's *Intimations of Immortality*. Those who think the poet wronged by time may be encouraged, and those who think that I should at least try to be more *avant garde* be scornful; as for myself I am surprised at this state of affairs, since I am not a Wordsworth fan. Where are John Donne and Gerard Manley Hopkins? I used to keep faith with them if no one else. I suppose that they have gone the usual way, with other poets, of dumps left in foreign places, and the weight of Wordsworth was always excessive for carrying about Aegean islands. However I did make him this compliment, that on my last day at home in England, with Amorgós in mind, I typed out to bring with me on four close sheets of quarto this one piece which during a last-moment flurry seemed indispensable.

Why? I cannot for the life of me remember why. No evening whim, the act of typing was carried out with all the deliberation of Dorset in my fingers, it was done at the last moment but had been intended long before, the purpose remained with me through the weeks in Athens and I am glad of it, but what gave the initial impetus I do not know. This may be the purging effect of living in Langátha, I like to write uncluttered with preconceived ideas, and curiously enough such pastoral English verse does not seem inappropriate to the place.

> *The rainbow comes and goes*
> *And lovely is the rose ...*
> *... Waters on a starry night*
> *Are beautiful and fair.*

This is a plain statement and Aiyiáli is a plain statement. The simple beauty of the first two verses reads well in a place which invites no purple passages. Aiyiáli may give a purple impression at the beginning because of the monumental style of its natural beauty and the harmony of the domestic, but purpleness has gaps to fill and I see nothing missing; purpleness does not deal entirely with the truth, and here everything is real and practical. I look up from my table and see a dazzling village — it does dazzle — terraced mountains opposite and a blue sea beyond, so calm today that it must be giving up fish in multitudes, and I may add that on a starry night these waters are beautiful and fair. To simplicity and beauty add sadness; one day I shall come back to congratulate the islanders on their new attainments and keep to myself that the things which I have seen I now can see no more.

I would like to make a guess about this work, that Wordsworth wrote the first two verses under the influence of the Muse — who is more real than a good many of the accepted forces in our life and at any rate a convenient means of reference to a state which certainly exists — that he discovered them on emerging from that state and decided that it was beholden on him to expand them into a grand Miltonian work. They pleased him, and be began to work upon a theory in which he vacillated, could not make up his mind, lost the flowing beauty of his inspiration, and although he did conclude in exultation he might as easily have stopped in doubt half-way. I like it rather the better for its key of human weakness, when much of it is hard on modern ears, and have gradually taken to the whole. We know and do not know, we make our philosophy and doubt, what is wonderful was once more wonderful, we look back and are inveigled on, and when all is said and done the irresolute may as well do his best to end triumphantly.

I have been watching the children about Aiyiáli, and since

childhood is the subject of the *Intimations* I think of them in conjunction with the ode. I really wanted to discover, if only as a mental exercise, whether I could possibly agree with Wordsworth's theory that 'Our birth is but a sleep and a forgetting,' that 'Trailing clouds of glory do we come,' as if our immortality — assuming that something about us is immortal — worked backwards, and that 'Shades of the prison-house begin to close' only when we have lived long enough to lose the aura of the heaven which we knew.

I cannot. I am prepared to consider any belief as feasible, and cannot see anything unreasonable in allowing this one the possibility of being valid when I come from a country where the conservative still follow a cannibal religion and the rest believe in all sorts of other improbabilities including nothing, which is the most difficult to accept or understand. However I cannot believe in backwards immortality. Since no truth of existence is within our comprehension I have to qualify all my sentences with a 'perhaps' or 'probably', but bearing these in mind I would say that Wordsworth was right about his children but not in his reasoning.

The child's religion is the world and everything that is real, first magical and then practical. The 'mighty prophet' brings these things to our attention by his faith in adult omniscience, requesting, 'Please turn on Andy Pandy' at the age of three and any time of day when he has deduced that the magician hand which turns the switch is responsible for the whole working of the television set. And I remember too, having been told that if I blew hard enough at traffic lights they would turn green, how I puffed from the front seat, sometimes performing the miracle with a whiff, sometimes turning purple in the effort, but always triumphing. I was six or seven when my mother disillusioned me, and it was a disillusionment which I accepted bitterly. My ability had seemed no more improbable than any of the other feats of life.

The children of Greek villages, without their traffic lights and television sets, are no more lacking in the mysterious, nor is there any basic difference between them and other children, for that age knows no formal barriers. Just as all human races have been born with laughter, so all children have been born with the same ways of self-expression, and seeing those of the Greek islands playing with those of foreign parents I call them not prophets but ambassadors. They are undeterred by lack of a common language and, more quickly than their parents, break down that barrier which is of little consequence to the intense interest of their play.

This is what I admire most in children — their absorption.

See where 'mid work of his own hand he lies
Fretted by sallies of his mother's kisses.

The language is not to our taste today, but it only means, 'look at him engrossed in his own work and irritated to distraction by his besotted mother'. The concentration limit of children of the youngest school ages is short, but only in their response to outside influence. Their private world is all-absorbing and not to be interrupted by grown-up routine. 'Have we had dinner?' asks my youngest niece, or, 'What did we have for dinner?' an hour before it is due to begin, and I am inordinately impressed by such detachment in a life which we have broken up decisively into compartments according to the times at which we eat. I am envious of the dreams.

I do not remember England before the age of six, for at the beginning of the invasion scare in 1940 when our house was requisitioned as a hospital, my mother responded to telegrams from relations in America, and there we went, to her immediate regret, to be marooned without transport home until 1944. My memories are chiefly of winters in Quebec, summers on the Island of Orleans, and the more I think of it, the more I am sure that size has its force in childhood.

I suppose it follows naturally that when one is smaller everything else is bigger, and yet I have the impression that if I was then half the height that I am now everything else was more than twice as tall. The woods on the island were boundless forests of trees so vast that they overtopped the Californian redwoods, and we 'pigmies' were somehow — that I knew — all-powerful, if only we could have found the key to the performance of those feats, flying and monkey-climbing and magic transformations that I knew we could achieve. And the whole of my universe was made more grandiose by the fact that somewhere there existed a place called England where everything was more beautiful than even our own forest, a place where we would all go eventually, and a man, a kind, good, loving man called 'Daddy' who was waiting for us there.

Postcards materialised almost every week for each of us, and once we received a record from him on which we heard his unsubstantial voice, a voice made more unearthly by the fact that for half the time he spoke in French. It was very wonderful and puzzling until the day when I put two and two together and asked my mother, 'Is Daddy God?' I had my proper religious education, we were headquartered in a bishopric, and all the evidence fitted perfectly. Far away was God and Heaven, and one day, when this thing called 'the war' was over, we would all go there, to the promised land.

If this Daddy were a more godly figure than my mother's brother who while we were living there was appointed Archbishop of Quebec, he must live in a paradise indeed. I have only two clear memories of my uncle during this period, once of his inciting us to recite dubious limericks over Sunday lunch when we were honoured by joining the grown-ups, and once of his shutting us up in the cupboard under the back stairs and growling like a bear outside, but I know that anything he did could only make him the more awe-inspiring. I was not at all surprised when he told me this last winter how he once performed a miracle on the island of Iona when he shook hands with an elderly clergyman who was at once cured of chronic sciatica and rheumatism. My childish conjectures were not so inaccurate.

Adults were a different species of people from ourselves, I was aghast at the first suggestion that a grown-up could do wrong. One day we too would turn into these superhuman beings, and I could have pictured it most easily had I been told that, like caterpillars, we would first wind ourselves into a chrysalis. '. . . And she was a lady,' Henry wrote with one decisive sentence for the denouement of one of many stories, 'and had a baby and a handbag.' That was it.

My sister Imogen, four years older than I, puzzled me. Nine is such a grand age when one is five. She was always half-way between me and the other world of grown-up beings, holding the answer to the secret of metamorphosis, and as I caught up so she went ahead, and so it seemed that it must always be. And yet at the same time we were static — I seemed unable to grow into another person, she remained a superior being, I inferior, while Henry in the middle could rise to her heights or stoop to my plane as he chose. We occupied, as it were, a train compartment and the world rushed past, but as one sometimes has the impression that it is the outside landscape that moves backwards rather than one's own vehicle that progresses, so I became aware of a new phenomenon: the stature of a person remains the same while the world grows smaller round him.

Whither it fled the visionary gleam?
Where is it now, the glory and the dream?

We acted a play for my mother on the island. Imogen, the avid reader, had no lack of plots for any theatrical occasion, and carefully instructed me in my role which required a swig of poison and dramatic death. A convincing stage prop was no difficulty, the bottle of poison-ivy lotion was clearly marked with the essential word, and therefore at the given moment I raised the bottle to my lips and quaffed it down. This is the simplest way in which I can explain that life is simultaneously magical and practical. The forests were gargantuan, they were the Garden of Eden with the lurking serpent, poison ivy. That was more than terrifying, it was evil, it once turned my mother into a bloated-faced woman whom I did not know; it added a fascination to what was otherwise so beautiful; it threatened to smite us throughout lifetime every seven years. We had a poisonous lotion to relieve it, and when I was required to drink poison I drank it. I was a princess and that was what the princess did.

'In five years time,' I said incredulously, 'I will be eleven.'

> *Why with such earnest pains dost thou provoke*
> *The years to bring the inevitable yoke?*

It was 1944. We went back to England with the first shipment of mothers and children from Canada, and in that year the world shrank. It was hard for England to be heaven under V-bombs, and harder still in the immediate post-war years when heroism was replaced by rationing. It was hard for my father to be divine, though once I had adjusted myself to his flesh-and-bloodliness I gradually discovered that he is often more masterly than God. Imogen went to boarding school, reappearing three times a year in glorious uniform and I continued to provoke the years. I went to boarding school and all that happened was that I remained the same while she was stately in the sixth form and became a prefect. I struggled on to reach the Elysian age myself — though not the status — to discover that there was nothing Elysian about it. I who had lived in magic forests and been a princess was only a fat girl with a loathing of lacrosse.

The age of the world's shrinkage lasts, more or less, a decade. It ends in agony, or so it seems in retrospect, for adolescence is abhorrent to me, but while I cannot say that,

> *The thought of our past years in me doth breed*
> *Perpetual benediction,*

I do think that the earlier ones are 'worthy to be blest'. When Imogen read who knows what eight-year-old logic into Dickens and finished all his books, when Henry, the architect, built cities such as gave me unquestioning faith in the validity of E. Nesbit's *Magic City*, and when I became enamoured of the stationer's, we knew our simple creed — delight and liberty. Then there were no inhibitions about covering as many of those virgin sheets as possible, no tearing up of paragraphs, no indetermination about what was a beginning, a middle and an end. 'Six hens, little hens, went to a boat. They explored it.' We had something to say and said it, and in the process gained nothing but enjoyment.

The children of Amorgós whom I know best are in the middle or the latter stages of the shrinking decade, and being in contact with them daily over lessons I thought that I might discover from them something which I had missed myself. Here, after the ambassador age, which is very young, they turn immediately into useful human beings, and those of Langátha seldom go down to swim in summer, saying, 'We have work,' and speaking unresentfully. English children are taken to the seaside and given donkey rides along the beach, and so would Athenian children be if any Greek could possibly consider the donkey as an animal of amusement value, but the children of Langátha are masters of a mule or two long before their heads reach saddle level. Michali's daughters swim almost every day only because they happen to have orchards by the sea, meanwhile as soon as they are old enough to wield a hoe they are unquestioningly useful in the fields. They reach adolescence far more gracefully than I did, and are, I think, happier than most English children who have more entertainment. Much as I should hate to be a teenage daughter of a Greek, I am often moved by admiration.

If they are happier, they are not so from placid involvement with their soil. 'The children of your island,' I told Costa, 'amaze me for their intelligence.'

'So they have brains?' he cried gaily. 'That comes on the wind. We live by the sea, we are islanders, there is nothing to stop the air that comes in.'

My youngest, newest pupil, is Michali, ten years old, his mother told me when she came to ask about the lessons, but I would have taken him for seven from the way he silently obscured himself behind her back while she, a short woman, was sitting down. He comes now clutching a new exercise book with all the important solemnity of extreme childhood, making an Everest of my staircase up which the distance that he must raise each foot for the next step shows what a mansion he reaches at the top to learn new shapes to make in writing, new noises to pronounce for what had been the ordinary objects and utensils of his life. He grasps his pencil like a workman taking up a hammer and uses it with the concentrated aim of a sculptor wielding a chisel. In three short lessons he has learnt the alphabet, though this is his first experience of the Latin characters, also one word beginning with each letter and to answer the question 'what is this?' with 'it's a knife', as if there were no trouble of innuendoes between 'this' and 'it'.

Michali is a great delight, and gives me the opportunity to take Vangeli free and let him share the lessons. Vangeli is Yorgo's younger brother, and while Yorgo at sixteen must often miss his English for work in distant fields or at the harbour, the treading of grapes or whatever the season may demand, Vangeli makes up for his losses by absorbing all that Michali can absorb, adorning my house with such beautiful dark eyelashes as seem to me good reason for wishing I were ten years old. Michali will be a successful grammar-school boy and engineer; Vangeli will win a scholarship, have more ups and downs perhaps and be an artist of some kind. I suspect that my staircase is higher to him than to his more practical companion, though it does not dumbfound his social grace. One thinks of them exactly as one thinks of any intelligent beginners and of their manners as the most intelligent. Yorgo too, diffident but not embarrassed, knocks on my door though it is open and he can see me inside, unless I call him first, and never leaves without a word or two of general conversation. Aiyiáli has its own awareness. He knows something, though he was never taught, 'Like this, like that, behave to foreigners.'

The little ones go to the primary school in Langátha, and at twelve will move on to the *Chora* where three classes are all that the island has to offer in the way of grammar schooling. Vangeli will follow Yorgo to complete his on Santorini, Michali go, I think, to Athens, while others go to Naxos, all depending on the placing of relations, hostels and the family finance. What are the children to do on Amorgós when they grow up? Learning is paramount.

The youth who daily from the east
Must travel still is nature's priest.

I do not know what Wordsworth would think of Nature's priest turning into a devotee of language. He is still the same child,

> *And by his vision splendid*
> *Is on his way attended,*

though I contend that the vision is what he himself created from the fabrics of the world. The priesthood for these children concerns their kindred feeling for the island, and unless Michali or Vangeli is an exception to the rule neither will have lost by Yorgo's age his enthusiasm for the learning or the home.

I always wondered what would become of twelve-year-old Irene when so abruptly flung upon the capital — a more upheaving step than my removal from Canada to England at the age of six. But schooling in Athens does not debar the island children from being island children, and when I met her this year on the boat I saw immediately that she had taken no other role to heart. Fourteen is such an awkward age, as I remember, such a mass of wayward complications, but apparently she had no inkling about that. She demolished the two-year interval by her well-timed reference to ice cream and was doing nothing worse than to make her family abandon village bread for a short time in favour of Athenian cottonwool. Otherwise I can detect no change in her except that she has learnt about four years' worth of English in the intervening two.

'Now you are here I am going to learn a big lot,' she informs me. 'Please, I need practice in the tenses,' or, throwing aside her current text book, 'this is very easy. Look, will you teach me some words?'

'What words, Irene? You're using new ones all the time.' She is, at an impressive rate, and makes a point of bringing them into conversation the next day. I know exactly what she is groping at. 'Perform a miracle, make me able to speak English as you do,' and so we do our best together, and when we discover that our lesson has flowed into a second hour she gathers up her precious notes and goes out to be agricultural again.

Nor do adult responsibilities confound the child in Irene. She goes off to the harbour at all hours of the night to use her English on incoming foreigners, and sometimes, while the family retire to Thollária, is left to cope alone with all the movement among the rented rooms. Her status is enlarged by her experience, but is not different. She usually spends nine months away, since Amorgós is so difficult a goal to reach for the short holidays at Christmas and at Easter, and yet it is the goal. The parental yoke is not easy to throw off, nor is there the slightest wish to throw it.

I asked her about dowries, a crucial issue in this family, and found her highly opinionated. 'Now I will can work and get my own money. I will not need. But,' she admitted, 'my father says there is something. Look, I don't want to take it. I will work and then I will can help my sisters.' If money in a family is for passing round that family she will not revolutionise the system. By diverting its direction she will gain great pleasure, but until she marries, in Athens or on Amorgós, she will remain the child of her parents.

Irene is fortunate. Yanni from a quayside *magazí*, with equal aspirations towards learning at sixteen, has to work to educate himself. He used to lie beside me on the beach, talking or not talking, very much a child in his confidence, and for the first fortnight of this summer when he was absent I thought that he had grown into his older brother who greeted me with shy disdain or not at all. But I realised my mistake as soon as the real Yanni was sprawled beside me once more on the sand, painfully skinny, white and burning like a fair-skinned foreigner at his second bathe, speaking with the voice of a treble suffering from a severe sore throat. He talked about his school in Athens, talked of his aspirations to go to university, admitted that he was not learning any languages. 'Why?' I asked him, 'Don't you want to? Most of the children here are learning now.'

He answered, 'I want to, but there isn't time. I work — furniture — I make furniture.'

Suddenly it became clear why his voice was rasping out in such a strident tone, it had been severed by the shriek of the electric saw. 'In the morning, seven-thirty till two, work. In the afternoon, four-thirty to seven, work — furniture. Then I go to school till ten o'clock.'

'And when can you study, Yanni?'

'Sundays. Look, I'm turning pink.' He looked at the cavity where most people have a stomach thoughtfully, 'Do you give English lessons?'

'Yes, a few.'

'How much are you paid?'

Oh Yanni, I thought, don't ask me to teach you English. Let the beach and your mother's kitchen be your summer hospital. I answered quickly, 'It depends. Where do you stay in Athens?'

'With my sister. But next year I'm going to be by myself. She is having a baby and there isn't any room. I shall be by myself.'

A lust for knowledge has certainly entered into the offices of nature's priesthood, but that is not out of keeping where lust is for enjoyment, and knowledge for the pleasure of knowing. Irene has this in spite of her serious scheming for the future, Michali and Vangeli have little else, but Yorgo does his duty.

Whither is fled, the visionary gleam?

If I know what that is, I saw most clearly at the age of eight. Shakespeare came into my life that year; I saw *Richard II* three times in quick succession, became infected by the words, inseparable from the book and spent my days learning passages by heart without one moment's attention to the unimportant fact that I was making bedlam of the sense. At nineteen I acted Portia and now I cannot recite even 'The quality of mercy' without stumbling whereas 'I'll give my jewels for a set of beads' will accompany me to my deathbed and beyond. Now my pleasure in Shakespeare comes chiefly from re-reading the plays in which I had some part before I was fifteen, and the complete works, which I brought with me two years ago, qualified first of all as 'words per bulk'.

Where is it now, the glory and the dream?

A great many of my most intelligent friends agree that Greece kills reading. 'I am always more interested,' said one of the English teachers in Chalkís, 'in the fly walking across the page than in the page itself.'

Then be interested in flies. I rather like their humming in the proper places, hanging about an open window on a lazy afternoon, even their siesta time strolling over the backs of my bare legs, I even enjoy that. Perhaps it is the poverty, which values detail, that increases one's awareness on this island. Growing less intellectual I lose sight of a division between the mundane and the spiritual; while small things are precious we are still overtowered by a precipice and I begin to live again in the dimension in which I lived on the Island of Orleans.

I have played into the hands of William Blake.

> *To see the world in a grain of sand*
> *And heaven in a wild flower,*
> *To hold the universe in the palm of your hand*
> *And eternity in an hour.*

This quality is surely one which Wordsworth recognised as well,

> *... nothing can forget the hour*
> *Of splendour in the grass and glory in the flower,*

and he saw it in childhood. To be childlike is not to be childish. Here, where there is the space to feel the size, I would be responsive and child-like again.

> *We will grieve not, rather find*
> *Strength in what remains behind.*

Damn it, I do not much like the final stanzas of the *Intimations*, nor, according to Wordsworth, do I agree with them, but if the verve and vigour of life come from seeing as we saw when we were ten then transparently we are saying the same thing.

My legs are growing goatlike and I overtake the mules who show more restraint about the upward way. Live every day to be your first. My religious education is coming back to me, to inspire my day with tinkering. On reconsideration I should say that 'childish' is a maltreated word, it should mean 'of a child' without scornful innuendo. That being established I can complete my day by saying, 'Now that I have become a woman I have not put away childish things.'

CHAPTER SEVEN

Astypálaia and the Mongrels

LAST week I went to Astypálaia. Twenty-five miles south-east of Amorgós it is the next stop on the itinerary of the summer boat, a three-hour journey twice a week. One might think it simple, and it sometimes is. When weather, inclination and the timetable are favourable at one and the same moment there is nothing easier than to go to Astypálaia one night and to come back the next.

The island is only eleven miles long, so if you should happen to find a co-operative water-melon seller there, an errand boy between the villages with a motor wagon, it is possible to do it minimum justice in a day. Its main village is one of the most notable in the Aegean, rising up to a thirteenth-century Venetian fortress which once housed — and with what higgledy-piggledy organisation of small streets and great noise — two and a half thousand inhabitants, nearly twice the entire population of the island now. The southern peninsula is mountainous, rather bleak, with oases of prolific orchards, already, before the middle of July, yielding figs and grapes.

Grapes! We do not have them yet on Amorgós, and *germádhes* — the cross between an apricot and peach that is juicier than either — ours have passed.

'Really?' the inhabitants look superior. 'Bah! Amorgós!'

The northern peninsula is a long, brown serpent winding through the sea with that low, rounded brownness which has nothing of the beauty of rich mountain brown; there is little to be said of it but its formation, so snake-like on the one Aegean island which has no snakes.

'No snakes?' my curious audience queried in Langátha on my way back home. The steps outside my backstreet grocery invite a lounging interval for whoever needs recuperation on the way up to the top. The smallest *magazí* with most to offer, Vassili's always overflows with leisurely wine-drinkers into the street. 'No snakes?' 'No, none. They once took one to Astypálaia and it died immediately. They can't live there. St Anthimos is responsible.'

There was nothing strange in my recounting the idiosyncrasies of their next-door neighbour to the inhabitants of Amorgós. There is no reason for them to go to Astypálaia, but they like to hear about it and especially about its weaknesses.

'Yesterday at midday I went to the beach below the village, which they all said was beautiful. I saw it from above and it looked fine, with trees along the back. That was what I wanted — shade; I was dead tired from the night before. Now I'm a wreck, I couldn't sleep one minute, it's all stones and dirt and ants.'

'Listen to that,' my audience nodded complacently to one another. 'What else did you find?'

'It was worth going to for the village, but otherwise there's nothing. I didn't want to stay.'

'Better here,' they all assured me, 'you're much better here.'

'But I ate figs and grapes.' I felt that I was doing the poor island down.

'So early?' they exclaimed.

'And water-melons are ripe too, and honey-dew.' I tried to do my best, but then remembered one devastating fact to cap the others, 'Retsina is fourteen *dracs* a kilo.'

The news descended quickly down the street while we ordered another four-drachma half-kilo at the standard price in Greece where barrels are in use. Now I must quickly say that I probably viewed Astypálaia, which I had heard of by report as beautiful, with the biased eyes of any Greek islander who always considers his own *patrídha* unsurpassed, and had the journey been the other way about I should no doubt have been able to report on the shortcomings of Amorgós.

What interests me, and what I most appreciate, is that these two chunks of land, rising so close together out of the same sea, are of such different character. In fact what I had done was not simply to make a twenty-five mile journey from one island to another, but to cross the line from Cyclades to Dodecanese, and this perhaps is why I was not greatly drawn to Astypálaia, I have seldom felt much in sympathy with the twelve islands. What with their proximity to Turkey and their recent Italian occupation they seem less like Greece than the Greece with which I am familiar, but I can hardly claim what seems to be the case, that geology understands political frontiers. Aiyiáli has a long beach of fine white sand — admittedly narrow, admittedly used by animals, but still fine white sand — and Astypálaia has a beach so grey and gritty that it is reasonable to call it dirt. Amorgós has olive groves, Astypálaia orange groves; Amorgós makes its own wine, and Astypálaia, which is ahead of us in the grape season, imports an expensive watery wine from Rhodes. 'This is the Dodecanese,' they say, 'it's different,' and yet Kalymnos of the same group has one of the best retsinas that I know, and if anything cheaper than that of Amorgós.

I like all this. I like the weighing up of different islands and the discovering of each in some way to vary from the others. I like saying to the Amorgots, 'Mykonos has no *germádhes* of its own,' and to the Mykoniots, 'On Amorgós the hens stop laying in August.' The moment that the seasons of each island are co-ordinated, and the moment that their sands are the same colour there will be no more reason for inter-island travelling in Greece.

My trip to Astypálaia, so simple once it happened, took a fortnight to achieve. It was during my first attempts to make it that our grocer shipping agent informed me, 'We do have a regular timetable these two months, only it may change days,' and I had to put it off another week. Somehow I was having an attack of Athenian excitability that night which had to be taken home immediately and written off. 'It is because of this that you have come to Langátha, this is why you chose this village in this district of this island. Were it not so — goddam infuriating that it may be today — you would not be here.' I am expecting my brother here in August, and vainly I had thought the week before that I had at last co-ordinated his flight with our boats. One should not be so confident.

If one 'has nerves', as the Greeks say, at being so insular it means that only half oneself is living here. Nerves are for the world from which we are divided; here, occasionally, an aeroplane cuts into our silence between Rhodes and Athens — what else intrudes? At night the sputniks move among the stars, and the television rays bounce between Europe and the Antipodes. How silly can you get!

'Have people been up there?' asked Costa, standing on my balcony one evening looking at the moon.

It was a rhetorical question, and he was much intrigued when I told him that they almost had, that it was scattered with objects let off from American and Russian rockets, and waiting for the tread of human feet.

'What is up there? What is it like?' he asked.

'It's all stones, it's the dullest place you can imagine in the universe.'

'Perhaps there are some minerals . . .' he began conjecturing, leaping in Greek manner to the lucrative point.

'Perhaps there are, but do you know the expense of sending one single rocket up?'

On an island with the prices of Amorgós the blowing up of so many million dollars sounds even more ridiculous than elsewhere. Costa waived the lure of minerals.

'But if it is all stones, why does it shine?'

With my slender knowledge of astrology, I told him all I knew of the sun's reflection and eclipses, moved on to gravity and space walking, and ended with a picture of the revolving world as seen from outer space.

Costa was moved, but the difficulty of obtaining unknown minerals dampened more enthusiasm than that which he could raise for fairy tales. We looked at it again. All stones. . . . It's beautiful from here. . . . Let it remain.

Astypálaia and the Mongrels 97

Lacking many things we are yet self-sufficient — we are also self-contained and self-controlled. We leave the things that do not concern us in their proper places and provide for our policemen a life that is extraordinarily lacking in event. Once I became almost anxious for our chief on this account.

'If you are tourist police,' I pointed out, 'you have only me to guard over, and if you are civil police what crimes do you find for a living? Do you get bored?'

He laughed and informed me that there is always work for a policeman if he wants it. He and his subordinate put up a string barrier when the boats come in. They control the hungry crowds on 15 August. I do not know what else they do. Perhaps we are peaceful for lack of newspapers. If those came daily the policemen might be busier, but once they get here they have lost their agitation value, or should have if one is properly in tune. Demonstration, assassination and all the other frenzied -ations which are influenza to the world are never borne to Amorgós, for the wind which blows in brain-power, as Costa says, is not a carrier of germs.

'This week we're shooting presidents, so let's go out and shoot a president,' but by the time we know about the new infection or find our president he will be out of date. So let us waive the privilege and look after our land. I shall make the most of this situation while I have it, knowing how in Athens I shall be amazed again. I cannot understand it, it greatly upsets me, when a thousand students from, say, A or B go out to smash C's windows because X has behaved aggressively to Y or Z across the world. The world is too full and too complicated. Listen, the world is too complicated. I shall be forced to talk about a house of cards, but not the upward kind, rather the series of doublets, the lean-to sheds in snake formation where — flick — there goes the first, and pong, pong, pong, the ripple floods down and demolishes the line. Who will be left to stand us up again? No one. There will be no outsiders. A, B, C, and X, Y, Z do not exist, we will all be one messy middle race marked M for mongrel.

I do not want to offend anybody about their mongrel dogs, who are often charming animals. I do not want to be offensive

D

about those who have gained by mixtures, for many of the finest people have emerged from melting-pots. Vagrants, in the good sense of the word, combine horizons. A vagrant and multi-lingual background is fine education for a child, and many of the greatest artists have had such a training and are truly cosmopolitan. What voice is richer than that of Maria Callas who speaks English regally? Our language is exalted by her usage, for it is flawless with European seasoning, it is the culture of Paris, Athens and Milan in London and New York. She, and all those who have the power of selection, whose ingredients are refined by wide horizons, are a part of all that they have met, and all those places are the richer for having given and received. But none of this has anything to do with what I mean by mongrelism, a process by which the world is turning grey.

Mongrelism is apparent on the quayside every time a boat comes in. Watching the unloading of the ferrying caïque I ask myself, 'Who are these passengers?' but the game of guessing nationalities has recently become more difficult. Clothes are more bizarre, faces are less interesting, and often what appears as a load of khaki-coloured Europeans turns out to be one hundred per cent Greek.

A remarkable fact that I have noticed in the last few years is that the middle-class provincial and Athenian tourists have not just changed their style of clothes and manner, they are beginning to change their skins as well as if they do so by reflection from what comes in to see the Parthenon. They are rejectors rather than accepters, and do not know the art of either role. They do not know the value of what they put on and what they throw away, and they are ignorant of their own ignorance.

Those who travel for the sake of being somewhere which they can call 'abroad' on postcards, those in whom the familiarity of their own background breeds contempt, and those who jump into a melting-pot where there are no ingredients to mix are no part of anything. A mongrel is what we used to call the noble savage once he caught measles from the missionaries and put on a second-hand shirt, that is how I use the word. He takes part in demonstrations from not knowing who he is — that really means he demonstrates against not knowing who he is — and if all places are not alike to him he wishes that they were.

'It's no good being sincere,' said Dame Edith Evans refreshingly in a television interview, 'if you can't be heard being sincere.' She thought that actors should be audible. Obvious that may seem, and yet she considered the present failure notable enough to comment on. Perhaps it is because few people know what to be sincere about. Can it be that in an era of uncertainty, of questions more than answers, incomprehensibility is creditable? Can incomprehensibility be still more creditable if cacophonous as well? Listen to the most popular pop singer, he has distorted all his vowel sounds, and distortion seems to have a frightening amount to do with the idiom of our age.

Comparing opposites is a way of clarifying problems. The idiom of the Victorians, for instance, has in a remarkably short time become almost the antonym of ours. We might say that they were probably ham actors, but I am sure that every word they spoke was clear. We might say that they were mistaken in thinking their own rightness universal, but they might also be justified — if they could see and hear them — in recoiling from our mongrel looks and voice. The precariousness of their existence in the early days of doctoring demanded consolation for the death-rate — a deep religious faith. The precariousness of our existence in the face of social mess seems to have demanded its rocky opposite. Faith, poor thing, which ought to be a virtue, often led to bigotry, and heaven knows where lack of it will lead. In Langátha I see social order, a people living somewhere between our two worlds yet thoroughly themselves, and from this temporary point of balance I can see no point in any way of living but by private decision and public tolerance.

I have a weakness for the Victorian novel, which was one of the best results of their rigidity. I am a Trollope fan, yet I seldom have the urge to read him on the beach. Books, like people, have their own right times and places, and I find that Dorset evenings are most appropriate for the Victorians. Trollope in a bikini is too incongruous. Therefore my range of reading becomes wider here, not only because of the accident of what books get packed. Even one's personal decisions can be geographical.

Let the people be catholic and the places insular, but if the people cannot be catholic let them stay where they are and be tolerant — better than being negative elsewhere. The inhabitants of Greek islands, those who stay where they are, are their places, and are tolerant.

This island is Amorgós, and the people who live on it are Amorgots. Katápola is not Aiyiáli, and Langátha is a long way from Thollária. A window is correctly *parátharo* in the *Chora*, but we, like peasants, speak of the *panátharo*. I once met an Amorgot girl in London — at the Savoy of all places — where she had some work as an archaeologist, and when I confessed to *panátharo* and the frequent eating of *fava*, which is vetch ground up with oil, she anxiously invited me to move over to her birthplace in the *Chora*, a different place beyond our mountain range. She is not by any means a mongrel, she has gained from all that she has met. She has published in German and is at home in Paris, and she likes her birthplace to be the *Chora* that it is.

I do not want to go to Astypálaia and find it Amorgós. I do not want to go to Athens and be living in New York. When I go to Istanbul I prefer to struggle with my fifty words of Turkish in incomprehensible bazaars than to be met half-way. If I were to travel farther East I should be disappointed if I saw no camels. If I came to England as a foreigner I should be disappointed not to have to master the handling of halfpennies and guineas and half-crowns.

I do not feel particularly at home in England, and there are many things about it which I dislike, but rather than make a cult of that I defend it for each characteristic that I see defensible, and nothing more. The climate, for instance, though distinctly gamma, is by no means the foggy epsilon that most foreigners make out at second hand. But chiefly I am thinking of what makes England England, and that must be what is English — obvious perhaps, but apparently it is what we are doing our best to eradicate.

On the whole we are an intelligent people, our rise to power in the past depended more on brains than brawn. Among other things we discovered very early how to count to twelve while others were confined to what they could calculate upon the fingers of their hands. From there we arrived at two hundred and forty as a convenient number for division and evolved a form of currency which allows more flexibility than the metric system and is also workable in daily practice — the English grocer can add up almost anything in his head.

The world, however, thinks in hundreds so we must think in hundreds. Goodbye, Britannia, you don't rule the waves today but you were a harmless institution all the same. Goodbye, guinea, and goodbye heavy, reassuring, convenient half-crown. You might have been put down as local colour in future days when all the world is grey. Welcome instead a great expense towards nonentity. 'But foreign trade . . .' they say, embarking on profound financial lectures which I cannot understand. My mathematics and my financial sense may not be strong, but I think I have enough reasoning power to see that any deal with foreign markets that is going to bring in the millions needed to cover the cost of transfer to a metric system will be conducted in nothing less than pounds. And into however many units each one may be divided you will still have to do the sum to find out how much that English pound is worth.

Gradually mongrelism spreads throughout the world, and everything idiosyncratic becomes a souvenir. If conformity confounds the laws of nature let them be confounded, and so we turn our clocks to Central European Time and please the continent by eating breakfast in the dark. It was accommodating of the British Government to make us do so, but they forgot to draw up the extra bill required, to be addressed to Heaven, 'God, arrange for the sun to rise in Scotland at the same time as in France.' I dare say that in their omnipotence they will soon find the means, and I dare say that very soon they will be sitting in chorus along the cliffs of Dover bidding the English Channel, 'Go back! Go back!' Or would they baulk at repeating a tradition in our history?

That channel has served us 'in the office of a wall'. Never fear, it is serving the same purpose now—to keep ourselves inside. We toe the line to accommodate the world and then we separate ourselves from the world by cutting our allowance of foreign currency to an extent that turns our island into a moated prison with wide entrance portals and the way of exit narrow, lined with obstacles. Are we driving towards world unity or are we not? We seem to be attempting both ways simultaneously and in each direction are given the less pleasant choice.

The English, before the £50 limit was imposed, had been progressing; we were no longer the most insular tourists in Europe, the worst speakers of foreign languages. The English coldness was becoming legendary and sometimes two of us would strike up an impromptu conversation in a train. But now that we are committed to such expense in removing the Englishness from England, we are supposedly deferring that future day when the ordinary man will cross the Channel easily again. By that time he may have regained his old frigidity, by that time travellers from other countries may be a little frigid too, for those who are still unshackled have their threats. The Greeks can no longer send money out of Greece, the Americans may have to buy their passports dearly, and I do not know what is happening to the natural laws of give and take.

The movement is going in the wrong direction, everything is happening the wrong way round. The places are becoming catholic and the people insular.

Driving up the Lycabettos with Peggy Glanville Hicks and seeing the hoardings rising at the top, looking down over the swamped remains of old Athens, picking out a survivor here and there among the international apartment blocks, I have the extra irritation of her comment, 'Thank God I've had my spree.' Would she exchange her fifty years for my thirty? Not on your life. To me she leaves the pleasure of witnessing another twenty years of mediocrity among a style of building as dreary as the theory of world government, where if one builder goes into revolt the result within one town plan is not original but incongruous.

This is the visual joy of the Greek islands, each one conforms to an architectural style within its own seacoast, and each is different. The houses of Skiathós are white with tiled roofs, of Skyros white with flat, grey roofs, of Mykonos all white, and these three types are repeated with variations throughout small Aegean villages, totally different in character according to the lie of land. Paros is the flattest, and therefore to me less interesting than others though it has won its own *réclame*. Elsewhere there is no room for monotony within the style, for every corner, every step, every degree of rising up a mountainside or thickening in whitewash makes geometric idiosyncrasy. Thus each village is an individual; take the boat and move on to another, it is somewhere else.

So, in spite of my annoyance on the grey beach of Astypálaia where I found beer in small, expensive bottles and no wine, I was mollified when told, 'This is the Dodecanese.' All right, I'll leave the Dodecanese to someone else, or if I come here be someone else myself. Those who are part of all they have met can be as many people as the places that they meet, and it will be inordinately dull when only one character is left. Amorgots, you would not know me if you could see how volubly I shall react from months among you when I move on to Mykonos, or how many miles I shall cover on the mainland later on. And, Julia, you would be astonished if you could witness my Langátha calm, but nerves belong to another person whom you knew — I am a chameleon, and I mean to go on being one.

It is better to be an optimist as long as that can possibly be managed, and I think that it can without evading hideous truths. Angry as I am in theory to think of what is being done I refuse to squander island happiness while the island is still here for being happy on. No one, surely, should spoil what he has for the sake of what he may be going to lose. So, islands of Greece and countries of the world, be kind towards chameleons. Go on being as many islands and as many countries as you are, and may there never be a snake on Astypálaia.

CHAPTER EIGHT

Pirates and Prostitutes

THE church of Ayia Triádha, the Holy Trinity, is the site of the old fortress of Langátha. It is visible below the village on the way up from the harbour, a miniature white patch on the daytime-grey and evening-red cliff face, but from directly underneath it is blotted out by its protective overhang; the flight of steps leads up, it seems, to nowhere or the sky. You then curl twisting up the spiral tunnel — it is most convenient to be under five feet from now on — with the feeling that the child-size portcullis may at any moment fall, and circle up on to a narrow ledge in the middle of which stands the renovated church. Does a little hacking out of a natural shelf allow this site to qualify for the term of 'fortress'? Well, it was used as such. And where did all the people stand? The problem is like that of putting the world population on the Isle of Wight, known to be possible, but difficult.

'When the pirates came, the people hid up there.' A teacher of the deaf who works in Athens and spends his summers in his native home, Langátha, was repeating the history one evening, and I could only feel that there would have been far less of a scramble if one part of the ledge had not been used up by a church.

'There was a day when the villagers were out reaping in the fields and a boy — they say a boy, but he was probably a man, a scout — had wandered down the valley and saw a boat come in. Men were disembarking, but they did not fly a pirate flag, he did not realise who they were until he saw them at close quarters coming up the hill. Then he ran to try to warn the villagers, but the pirates were overtaking him. He took out his pipe and played a tune on it — a message. The villagers heard and understood, they ran from the fields, climbed up into the fortress, let down the portcullis and began boiling oil ready for the attack. There was a battle and the islanders beat back the pirates. But the boy was killed before he reached the top. The pirates left him by the path and shoved a rock on him — you know the one? It's half-way up the track — they call it *mirízondas*, 'smelling', because of course the next day or the day after there was a bad smell, and still the flowers which grow around it have a special scent.'

What I had always felt when I was told this story was that if I had been a pirate I would have gone off and plundered the village quietly while the people were sitting so remotely on their ledge, instead of charging up the cliff into the reach of boiling oil and rocks. But I have discovered that while the age and calling of the scout is a subject of opinionated argument, the words 'pirate' and 'Turks' are used indiscriminately to cover invaders or pillagers of of any kind. This lot were not after treasure, they were devastators of the population, and such scenes certainly occurred. The 'smelling stone' is already one of the recurrent themes of modern Greek legend; now I was doing my best to extract some sort of date.

'Many many years ago,' the teacher said. Now I know that 'many many years ago' in Greece dates Agamemnon, Pericles and Byron, so I prompted him, 'About . . . ?'

'Oh, at least eighty years or a hundred,' he exclaimed.

I could not have been more delighted. Why, considering island longevity this is almost within living memory, and all these villagers sitting peacefully round the *platía* lamenting that they have no electricity had parents or grandparents always on the alert to leap up to the rock, let down a portcullis and stoke up a fire for the tormenting oil.

'That is why the girls of Amorgós are the most beautiful in the East,' the teacher said. 'They are descended from pirates and prostitutes.'

I did not ask him, 'How far East?' or 'East of what?' but he was right in saying that the beauty of these girls is famous and their fame is justified. The pirates were strong by nature, the prostitutes had to be beautiful to earn their living, and the pirates came here. 'Strength and beauty,' he repeated, hardening his biceps, 'a pure stock'.

I like to have had a link provided with these marauding figures who are growing into legend rapidly, and almost into legendary heroes. They certainly had their effect on the topography of island villages, and I am much divided in my mind as to whether the present state of affairs would be improved if the old threat had not lurked. Langátha, Thollária, and Potamós could be one thriving town around the seaside plain, and so it would be on all Aegean islands whose principal beauty is at the top of what is hot to climb in the season when most foreigners abound. Then many dying villages would be uprising, then perhaps the exodus would be less great to Germany, and Mykonos — preserving more of what it was — would share with its jealous neighbours its huge allotment of the fortune that has come into this country in the last ten years. But if Langátha were not so far up its hillside there would be no mayor's house at £3 10s a month. I like the village, I am grateful to the pirates.

'We have no road,' the teacher said. 'If there were cars we would have tourism.'

'I have heard that one and a half million drachmas have been made over. . . .'

The teacher rocked with laughter. 'Where have you heard that?'

'They say so at the harbour.'

'They see it in their dreams. Nikita, did you hear that? They say that one and a half million drachmas have been given us for a road,' and everyone around the *cafenion* was rocking too.

'We need progress,' said the teacher. 'Progress is always good.'

Always? It depends what progress is. I was feeling very cautious about progress because I had been reading Alan Moorehead's *The Fatal Impact*, and was particularly shaken by one sentence about the aborigine. 'In Australia there had been no need for him to develop.' I could not read on without a jolt. If the human being was born only for existence, and if four possessions can be sufficient through the year, for the man a spear and throwing-stick, for the woman a digging-stick and bowl which, when she has nothing to put in it, will serve her as a hat, then 'progress' from the sins of Adam to spacemanship are the trappings which we heap upon ourself in our struggle to exist.

We do not have the climate of the aborigine, we would be cold with his possessions and no more. But such an ominous word as 'trappings' cries out for caution when the world we live in is an early work.

Bad taste was the second of the sins of Adam — it must have been unless the wrecking of beauty through so-called progress is a world-wide coincidence. How else can this saddest of all facts be true, that the state of perfection once reached, as near as can be, has no course but to go into decline? Mykonos deserved its fortune and having reached its zenith grows less beautiful. This would hardly matter if it were exceptional, but it is not, it is typical of the rule. Our world is an early work, right leads to wrong. All that has become wrong about beauty spots stems from what initially was right.

'Progress is always good.' But what is progress? Go from Mykonos to Delos, see the delicate mosaics, the columned courtyards and the frescos, the well in every house, and you cannot say that progress is necessarily an advance in time. I do not believe that the poor lived then in more discomfort than the poor of Greek villages today, or very differently. There was slavery, but its abolition cannot justify all the backslidings of our time.

When I took Vangelio's room in the *platía* here in April I rejected its progressive sanitation — an attempt to imitate with pipes what had been seen elsewhere — in favour of the truly primitive. Behind the mayor's house is a small shed built of stone with raftered ceiling, whitewashed, with no door but facing the blank wall of another outhouse so that one enjoys the open air in privacy. There is a shallow step at the back, like the step up to a regal dais, and a hole in the middle from which in midsummer no suspicion of a smell exudes. Water is as unnecessary here as it is ineffective where amateur pipes have been installed, but pipes, like mainland television, mean the later 1960s, and therefore are called progress.

When I am in England I enjoy good television, though I never miss it elsewhere and I abhorred Greek television when I saw it for the first time on Salamis this spring. What must formerly have been a friendly café-restaurant became a hushed temple doing honour to the noise of an out-dated series of American films with spasmodic subtitles which nobody could read. I do not mean that the audience were illiterate, though some may have been, but in a large room subtitles of television size cannot be read for many hours, or many minutes, even by those who have an unrestricted view, and no one who concentrates so long is doing himself much good.

But progress, says the teacher, is good.

I would not deny you progress, but I wish that you could receive it a little more artistically. It is a denial of itself when the second stage is inferior to the first and that is what happens when it turns into a rocket for those who have not seen a steam engine, or the television for those who have not read a book. I wish you could see it as a development and not a division from the past. Soon you will be forgetting that your looks were inherited from the strength of pirates and the beauty of prostitutes.

The teacher uses 'civilisation' as a synonym of progress and is thinking largely about objects. I find this rather frightening. For how without disaster can end-products be handed to whole races who have not seen the earlier stages? The way from headhunting to Hiroshima is very long, even the way from piracy to S-bend pipes is better taken slowly. This is not a matter of prejudice but one of feasibility, and I believe it firmly, anything can be given to individuals — and many are able to accept — but 'civilisation' is not a commodity that can be handed to a people without the history in which it grew. It is not possible, and whether or not this is unfortunate no country can pass on to another the stages of its history, telescoped, précied, on a plate, in any way.

If progress is not made through history, history might as well be cancelled from the timetable, and nations lose their memory, but they will not be civilised. For how can we move on from A to B, weeding out and rearranging, if A has been abolished? Not in a straight line. Rather, as we set out in dodgem cars to hit the elusive target, the subject will have changed to one of drunken progress.

The Greeks by common practice admit the past when it is useful, flourishing the names of their forebears of the Golden Age as a badge entitling them to manœuvre conversations to their own advantage, or remembering Byzantium when they feel possessive towards Istanbul. It is not tactful to speak enthusiastically of Turkey, but praise of the *polis*, which is Constantinople, 'the city', is taken as a compliment.

'Of course it's beautiful,' said Artémis, a fisherman of Mykonos, 'it's Greek, and it has Ayia Sophia there.'

The fact that Ayia Sophia is preserved as a bare and gaunt museum whose domes are daily echoing with the call to prayer from the minarets of its encircling mosques did not deter him, for apart from buildings there are the people, and the city is full of Greek inhabitants. Well, I admitted, I did hear a good deal of Greek about the streets, but in fact there are rather more Turks there than any other race.

Bah! They will leave, and inevitably I was to hear repeated the prophecy about the six-toed Constantine. Can it be fulfilled, I wonder, while the king is kept in exile? Reject the man, preserve his toes, and have the city back.

'In two or three years, five at the most,' Artémis promised, 'the Greeks will have regained the city. You see, it was our own before.'

'In that case,' I suggested, 'you might say that the Turks should come back into Macedonia, if not farther still.'

Ah, but before there was Alexander, and he conquered this and that and that....

On this basis we should have a field day with ancient and

modern atlases. Should England claim half of France again, or should we go farther back and declare England to be a Roman province, breaking up Italy into a mass of small republics? According to Artémis we should stop exactly at the point most profitable to the Greeks. 'So,' he repeated, 'within five years we will have regained Constantinople. And not by war, not by bloodshed, quietly.' And how will that be done? 'We will do it by diplomacy.'

This is most impressive considering who are the Greeks and who the Turks. 'And in the same way,' he added to fill his cup of happiness, 'Cyprus will be ours as well.'

I could not bring myself to mention that by his previous reasoning the Greeks would have a flimsy claim to Cyprus, for he would doubtless have been able to produce some new ingenuity of argument to topple mine. Artémis is an extreme case of those who distort the past for the purposes of the present, but there are probably as many extreme cases as any others in the world. We like to hear that the ancient names are not forgotten, we have been using them in England lately to make fine speeches about the 1967 April revolution, and as wildly as Artémis.

Idealists profess themselves outraged by a military dictatorship in Greece, 'the birthplace of democracy'. If by Greece they mean the city state of Athens they are right in as far as it was the birthplace of the idea of democracy, a form of government which in practice was founded by dictators, short-lived and based on slavery. The colonels might be considered as the descendants of the tyrant Pisistratus who paved the way for Pericles, in which case they would be doing well — it is on the outcome of a military takeover that judgment must depend.

One dictator turns out to be an Attaturk, another Mussolini. The beginning of dictatorship, which is a well-intentioned cleaning up of messes, is no pointer to the place that it will take in history. But like military government or like it not, one might as well remember that Greece has had eight such revolutions since 1922 as remember Pericles, and call the latest one not inappropriate. It would be kinder to the peasant who has no say in the matter to see it from that viewpoint than to keep our pounds or dollars from his pocket by high-minded absenteeism.

When the offended foreigner dictates what he would like to be the outcome of the future, it seems that he does not realise how little experience the Greeks have had of monarchy, nor that the crown which Constantine inherited had little precedent of peace. The English royal family can trace its ancestry back to King Alfred and beyond, the Greek royal family cannot produce one drop of Greek blood. The one is a part of its own country, the other an extraneous gift. I would like to see the return of the exiled Constantine, but I would never, even if it were my business, agitate to say that this must be. In the same way I would be privately sorry, if it were not my business, to see the English monarchy disappear. Here we are back at mongrelism, another denial of the past, for since we cannot even talk about our sovereigns and governments in the same terms, how can we conform on details?

If progress depends on history we cannot be world-wide conformists, minders of other people's business and forgetters of our own. It is not practical when our best habits are each founded on our own most solid institutions which worked from the beginning because they suited different climates, different temperaments. The English monarchy, for instance, in danger of becoming as isolated as the Acropolis, needs some fortification such as a House of Lords and public schools. Since these also educate their children rather well it seems a pity that they should be in jeopardy.

My father, bound for Winchester, began learning Latin at six, and I do not suppose that that has been a disadvantage to his life. A six-year-old mind is methodical, it likes rules and regulations, laws and logic, it may even enjoy its historical heritage — a pompous phrase perhaps but exactly what I mean, for history, unless I am much mistaken, is something in which we are involved today. Being rather soft myself I do not mean that Latin and logic need include cold baths, brimstone and treacle and all the spartan habits that used to be thrown in — I think that the Spartans must have been a most unattractive race — but I cannot call it progress when I notice that equally intelligent children of the same age today can hardly write a letter in their own language comprehensibly. My Utopia is Latin with central heating, or, if you prefer it, French, for movement and advance include much change, but mongrelism, which fears singularity, wants to eliminate the starting-point.

Whether or not this has happened can be judged immediately by manners. I would prefer to live in Athens, which one often feels still to be a village, than in London, and yet I sometimes think that London manners are superior. Now this is strange because the country Greek is one of the most gracious beings on this earth. It can therefore be deduced that in coming to the metropolis he calls it the epitome of progress and utterly denies the ethics of his grandfather — the ethics only, not the man himself, for he is probably supporting him financially.

The Golden Age, we must admit, is separated from him by fifteen hundred years of revolution, civil war and foreign occupation. He is the descendant of the Turkish occupation, not of the city state. England, which has not seen a foreign army on her side of the Channel since William the Conqueror came from Normandy, has had, in spite of all upheavals, a greater sense of continuity, more time to chew on new developments. That is why we are the better ordered about litter and spitting — two minor details by which one can judge the progress of a race.

I really must stop speaking disparagingly about the Golden Age. Golden it was, and tempting for us to say, 'If only it could be....' The slaves were not badly treated, and sometimes I conjecture whether such a system could be workable with paid employees in their place. I like the city state, I like the smallness of it, so utterly opposed to mongrelism. There is no doubt that in the fifth century B.C. something very near to perfection was attained. But that, as Kitto in *The Greeks* expresses very clearly, was the death bell of the state. Once we have started moving we cannot halt again, and perfection has nowhere to advance. Right, I said, leads to wrong, and only the aborigines who have never moved at all can stay contented or discontented where they are. Those

The 'Mayor's house' in Langátha

The author looking across Langátha from the Mayor's house

Catherine and Jason at Aiyiáli beach

Village steps in Langátha

Langátha, view from the Mayor's house

Irene Stephanaki (left)

Costa in his orchard

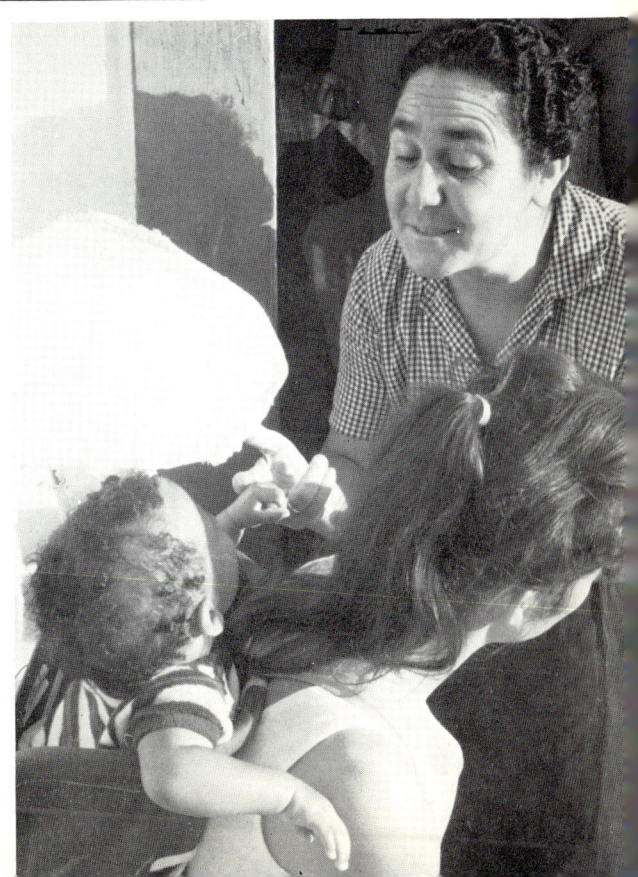

Vassili's wife with Jason and Catherine

The priest of Langátha

Michali and Vangeli

The feast of the Panayía

who have assumed the sins of Adam can only expand on them again.

We must move; we cannot help it. For all my liking of the guinea I am not conservative, but I want to preserve out of the holocaust whatever has proved good. Living in the past is one of the conventional sins of our confusing era, but it is quite a different matter from making the past live in the present — to do that one need not be conservative or retrograde. We must not deny the past, neither must we distort it, but we can make use of it.

I live in a hill village, and I am using the past for the purposes of the present. I am taking advantage of the pirates, I am influenced by the mayor. I am affected by his career, aware of him in domestic details. He is my business.

He built among other things the best well in this part of the village, in the middle of the old kitchen beneath my living-room. Once a scene of great activity from which dishes were carried in all weathers through the courtyard and up the outside stairs, it has become the silent home of spiders; the stone sink and the open fireplace have been unused for many years. Many years! I use the term like a Greek peasant, for no one can tell me much about the house. Though the mayor was the grandfather of Costa's sister-in-law and it was not much longer than a decade ago that the family moved out, he is a legend now. Yet whatever survives from the legend has proved good and I am much afraid of losing the smallest part of his most useful monument, the headstone of the well.

The roots of the apple tree growing on the nearside of the courtyard and rising up above the balcony before the door have burst the stone sides, the water has escaped, and I am faced with crisis as each day the murky scrapings become more difficult to draw. Costa tells me that he will repair the well 'after the Panayía', which is how we measure time in summer, before or after 15 August. He will then rip out the headstone and climb deep down inside, and I have faith that he will emerge again alive, but will he replace the stone as it is now? It is rounded with inch and two-inch grooves which the rope of my own bucket must wear as deep again as that of any former kitchen-maid, and these make drawing easier. Suppose, when Costa attacks it with a pickaxe it should be broken up? But we have made a sculpture of the stone with rope.

Meanwhile the greedy apple tree is dying, and I am afraid that we may lose that too. Its fruit is never larger than an almond and therefore, Costa says, it is 'no good', but I like to see the topmost leaves of the offender blowing just outside the door. Trees, like institutions, take decades and centuries to grow again. I wanted to tell him to be thoughtful about the quick cutting-down.

Now that the water level is sinking daily Costa says that I must fetch a supply from the public drinking-tap. Sometimes when I am feeling virtuous I do, but this is at the very bottom of the village, and by the time that I arrive home with a shoulder aching beneath the weight of my earthenware water-pot I usually decide that my own water, clear as soon as it has settled, can go on doing me no harm. My shoulder, unfortunately, was not inherited from pirates.

This expedition often leads me to the farthest *magazí* where the landlord's wife is in need of kind words and comforting. She went to the festival of Ayia Paraskefí last week, a good three hours beyond Katápola, fell off her mule and broke her arm. I found Costa and the carpenter here the other night listening to her lamentation over pain and the inability to work.

'Thank God,' we said, 'that it wasn't the right arm. Then there would have been *klámmata* — tears and cries — indeed.' This provoked a long discussion about right hands and left. Costa asked, 'Do left-handed people write from right to left?' and I said no, but Arabic goes from right to left and left to right, and very soon we were scudding among a variety of foreign scripts.

'So that,' said Costa, the proverbial Greek in being interested in information, 'is why we have the expression "like Chinese".' All such conversation is as provocative and unpractical as speculation on the moon, and it prospered on very good retsina whose quality, the carpenter assured me, was partly due to the barrel which had been made a hundred and fifty years ago.

'It's good wood,' they said with the eclectic tone of connoisseurs, and I, agreeing, told them how on tourist islands nowadays the wood is turning into glass, that we in our poverty were drinking better stuff than what one drinks on Mykonos for up to twice the price. Retsina in fact is going the way of the poor English kipper, which has no reason to be sneered at but that it is cheap, while beer is on the upgrade because of its expense. Mykonos, which knows better than Aiyiáli what to do with telegrams, is forgetting what to do with wine, forgetting that by force of nature — since history and geography are bound together — England grows the hop and Greece the grape. Costa, who in practice minds his own business and the business of his grandfathers, would not have thought otherwise. 'Good wood,' he said ,'good wine.'

He provoked a thought which made me suddenly elated, 'That barrel is contemporary with the pirates.'

CHAPTER NINE

Jimmy and the Nightingale

WHEN I was congratulated on my Greek one evening by an Athenian visitor the villagers retorted, 'But she's educated. Educated people know all the languages.' The myth, which is recurrent in this country, has been to some extent exploded here by my disinclination to teach French because, as I explain, 'I make mistakes,' and they, a little puzzled and disappointed, giving the air that my refusal is due to modesty, have had to agree that it is logical.

'She's educated. She's an author.' Probably all educated people write books as well. In any case the state excuses me for some of my eccentricity in occupying the mayor's house by myself, a way of living which by rights should fill a self-respecting woman with terror and loneliness. Yesterday I met old Marco's daughter, a young Athenian mother who has just arrived here for the summer, staggering up the mule track as I was coming down. On seeing me she reeled thankfully against the wall.

'Come and sit beside me, Carolina, I'm alone. What shall I do? I have no mule, it's hot, it's all uphill — I can't.'

'It's the coolest day for weeks,' I tried to soothe her.

'But Carolina, I'm alone.'

This was the greatest of her hardships in walking up the mule track, and one which obliged me to look shameful at my answer when she asked if I was living in the same house as before, and by myself. 'Aren't you afraid?' she asked. They all say this, every one of the women, and when I ask, 'Afraid of what?' they think a bit and then suggest, 'Suppose some person came . . . ?'

'Here in Langátha? Who? And what should happen?'
They are always floored by this and always end in peals of laughter to think of anything that could threaten or prove dangerous. But what about the evenings? How do I pass the time?

I don't, it does the passing by itself. My lamp is often the last to go out in the village, and that would hardly be the case if I were bored alone.

The answer which I ought to give to satisfy completely, though so far I have not been able to bring myself to make it, is, 'I'm educated.' This would be interpreted as, 'I belong to some strange esoteric group where we read books and are immune to all sorts of human weaknesses.' Of course I don't agree because I have more human weaknesses than they, but it would dispense conveniently with longer explanations.

'If I had company, how could I follow my work?' This is unanswerable, and I am almost as impressed as they, since I am only hermit-like in spasms, then I walk home alone to light my lamp and wonder what has made so natural the train of circumstances which has led me to a house and village without one other foreigner.

Let me make this clear, I might equally have said, '. . . which leads one person to a place where no other of his kind has stayed.' I am 'a person', and like all people I know nothing of the world but what my own eyes see, my own ears hear, and what I feel with my hands. I cannot say, 'Yorgo sees a beautiful blue sea,' because for all I know what Yorgo sees may be a muddy green. I cannot speak for anyone but myself.

This truth immediately confronts me with a problem which has been with me from the beginning of my thinking life, that each individual is somehow a possessor of the universe. If the world as we each know it is only as we know it by our own five senses, the existence of the world is our own existence, it began in the first years of our memory and may be blotted out at any moment, it is here, inside our heads, a little way back from our eyes, quite unmistakable. And what are we to do about it when we each revolve on our own bone?

*There is wonder in the universe
And in the cracks of small places under the earth,
And every jot, every tittle to be reflected
In my eyes,
Beaten against my ears,
Tasted by my tongue,
Pressed into my skin,
Into my own self,
There congested, ruminated upon and for the most part rejected.
I on my own bone revolve.*

One's juvenilia, which seem wonderful only at the time of writing, do occasionally hit on some idea that is worth thinking about again in adulthood. How can one know the size of one's own universe? What is one to do about all that which one's capacity rejects? What would Van Gogh have seen on this mule track that I have missed? Of all the impossible experiences that I should like one is half a day in which to borrow those eyes and see the colour of his universe. He comes to mind before any other because of his painting of trees with the perception that should always be given to the undersides of olive leaves, and because of his painting of a chair, when here the beauty of existence is emphasised by what is menial. But while Van Gogh's eyes would have seen wonders in Aiyiáli I am restricted to my own.

I cannot understand why anyone should make the conventional exploration of the world to find his own identity, or else by meditation and self-analysis search to find out what he is. I do not know why anyone should 'know himself', I hardly know why he should be told 'to thine own self be true'. The relationship of one person to his own self cannot be important, nor do I see that the world can prosper by the private possession by anyone of goodness. If I explore myself I only do so to explore the world, and these two maxims have only one meaning to me, they make sense only if they have this meaning, 'Know yourself to know the world,' and 'be true to the world which is yourself.'

When I was asked in Athens about the subject of my book I

could never give more than a vague answer because I was not sure of it myself. I only knew that the more I laboured over my translation and the longer I lounged about at the Phengári the more the process of being sociable and busy was aimed at Amorgós. I was straining for the right moment to sit down at the mayor's table, because, like a sculptor whose block of stone is ready, I knew that mine contained a statue ready for the careful chipping and release. But once I was challenged when I made the metaphor, 'If the statue is complete, why not leave it there?'

I was dumbfounded by the question because it asked me, why do publishers exist? Why are there picture galleries and concert halls, why are plays produced? It asked me, why do writers write and painters paint? An answer was rather a lot to take upon myself.

So I did not give one then. I thought about it, and that night at the Phengári I used the back of my cigarette packet to make the statement, 'But my statue has wings.'

My metaphors were more than obviously mixed. I might perhaps have said, 'My statue sings,' because I had been thinking about Keats' nightingale whose relegation to the wastepaper basket was a great problem to me all that day. However, I think that would have sounded stranger still, and I shall stick to what I said. I wrote it down with great conviction and the meaning is one in which I still believe.

I did not mean that my statue was a good flier, I meant that that was its function, that is what it is supposed to be. And certainly if, in theory, I could achieve a nightingale I would not throw it into the wastepaper basket, I do not think that the proper place for nightingales any more than a box is a proper place for a Pietà, and I do think that a writer who has intercourse with no one but wastepaper baskets must have the biggest ego of us all.

The question which Marco's daughter raised of solitude, though she did not know why, was a crucial one. The writing of books is an intensely lonely occupation. Not only is it done, like the other creative arts, alone, it never has an audience. Sentences are composed, each word is important, and readers say, 'How nice' about the whole, or, 'I enjoyed your book.' The theatre is teamwork, the concert hall is teamwork, even a picture depends partly on the hanging, the style of a room and its relation to other ornaments. A book in this sense is the least symphonic of all artistic works, neither the process of working nor the detail of the finished article is truly shared, yet still the writer has to try to share his universe.

Reconsidering my message, in whatever state its metaphors may be, I have come to the conclusion that I was correct in writing it. I need hardly add the qualifying 'in my opinion' here, because when the wings were tied and could not fly I physically rejected Greece, the reaction was of the body which decided to opt out of living here, and sadly factual. I can also date to the minute, with a greeting on the quay of Mykonos beside Bouboulina's statue, the factual moment which led to a season in which life was complete, and to understanding of what a full life is.

It was three years ago, the greeting came from Jimmy O'Connor and was casual. 'Hullo, Carolina.' — 'Hullo, Jimmy,' I had known him so well and no better for two years, but it involved me in one of those influential accidents that make one feel that there is something very business-like about the timing of the events of life.

He had drawn up tempestuously in his Landrover, and emerged with locks of Irish hair more than usually distraught and a large foolscap package in one hand. My own hair was probably awry as well from impatient urgency in extreme heat, and I was carrying a typewriter. I had come off the boat the night before, slept I can't remember where, and could not contemplate waiting for the later bus to transport my baggage to the beach.

Jimmy said, 'I have to send a T.V. script to London and the only typist on the island has given up.'

I said, 'I'm wondering how to get my typewriter to Platí Yialó.' If we had had a rendezvous we could not have made our approach to Bouboulina with more highly co-ordinated steps.

Half an hour later I was on my way, the rest of my luggage sat in the Landrover outside the O'Connors' country house while the machine was being put to use inside. At half-past one I typed the final sentence. Nemone stopped hovering with ouzo, and we drove down to Platí Yialó to celebrate the occasion, dripping in bikinis, with lunch at Petinos' taverna which was to be my base. I did not know then how important it was to celebrate the fact that my arrival into the Greek summer began with four hours' continuous work instead of back-slapping on the beach. I suspected that the O'Connors were becoming among the best of my foreign friends in Greece — they demonstrated that again last year when they helped to lay me in a disintegrated condition on the boat. In some way they are connected with the beginnings of a flight and fall, and only by looking at such situations can I understand something of writing and of life. I know no other reason in a writer for exploration of the self.

I was soon called back to the O'Connors' house. Nemone, who writes under her maiden name Lethbridge, had work for me as well. *The Portsmouth Defence,* the first play in her television trilogy, was ready to be typed, and it revolved through my machine alternately with the first pages of Jimmy's *Three Clear Sundays,* and the piles rose in quadruplicate and the house became a factory until each cool and conversational lunch hour and sometimes afterwards. I am not sure about the correct sequence of those plays, that summer session blurred into the next one and I was still typing them. This was the month before I came to Amorgós, and one of the best months in my life.

Life and Greece and work were one and the same thing. I was living two minutes from the beach in what became known as 'the cowshed', getting up at five every morning for two hours' first-draft writing of the final chapters of *The Mad Pomegranate Tree,* walking half an hour with the typewriter — how it shunted to and fro — to the O'Connors' where I engrossed myself in their work. I learnt the pleasure of refusing round-the-island boat trips — 'No!' cried Nemone and I in unison — and was yet by no means unsociable. I swam, talked, listened, spent half the night in the village, walked back in the early hours and got up at five again. I thought, the human body is a great machine, it is a battery, as you drive it so it charges and the further you drive it the more strength it gains. If one is a writer one has to be a whole show in oneself. If the universe is in me I have to be the universe, and that is all that I can do about it when I revolve on my own bone.

During that time I came to understand how basically work is part of living, and sharply developed a dislike of the question, 'What do you do?' which inquires evasively about finances, pushes the world into categories with its meaning, 'How do you support yourself?' Writing was a part of living and what I did was live. As for, 'Are you gathering material?' that is the worst of all. I gather mulberries, I gather figs, I do not consciously detach myself to gather material from the trees. My material is living, if I had to go out and gather it that would be because I hardly live.

I cannot think of any more appropriate couple than Jimmy and Nemone O'Connor in which to make these discoveries. She is immaculate in voice and face from Oxford, he 'a bit scratchy' from twelve years on Dartmoor. She is a barrister and he a convicted murderer. His range of subjects includes criminal lunatics at Broadmoor of which he writes from inner experience, and she writes of law courts from experience at the other end. In combination they are a history, and both are passionate in what they write, scarred perhaps by his unproven innocence — he is among the most scrupulously honest people that I know — but cool in judgment too. I learnt a lot about dimensions in their house.

'Goodbye, little waif,' said Nemone one day as was her habit, and then corrected herself, 'No, you are not a little waif any more.' Since she too had seen a metamorphosis something must have happened, I understood about the wholeness of life and work. It was only a few days before I left for Amorgós that she made this observation, so it was propitious for my arrival here, and I had the best prelude possible. The mayor's house in Langátha is not for little waifs.

The mayor's house is a place for being self-contained, for containing all the parts of life, and it is Greece. When a year later the madness of the pomegranate remained unjustified, and if I had come back it would have been to face Costa with my failure and be a waif again I would have ceased to write and ceased to live. I nearly did. My statue had no wings and I was ill. It was then that the O'Connors stood among my friends who put me on the boat from Mykonos to go defeated back to England, and I did not return to Greece until the shift of balance came and the pages which had pleased Costa were in proof. Jimmy and Nemone themselves had played a part in this development, so the moment had become more than ever historic in my life when we collided with typewriter and manuscript, but why this country rather than another was involved I am not sure.

I do not believe that one is fated to any course beyond its type, but I do believe that one is responsible for the place and timing of influential accidents, that life is composed of little else and that when one is receptive they happen well. I have often provoked them to happen very badly and distorted them afterwards into situations which they were not supposed to be, but as long as one listens while one goes along one will end up in much the same place, if it is the right one, despite all the apparently diverting side-tracks on the line. All artists must live somewhere and it is one of their problems to find the place that suits them — or the place they suit.

I cannot call my finding of Langátha accidental for I worked so hard at it, but it depended on the accident of my first coming to Greece. And that one, if only for its leading to this village as a base of exploration, has proved the best that I have allowed to take me where it will. In any case when writing was no part of living Amorgós was no part either, nor was Greece, and I was part of nothing, I had lost my universe. All cogs of a machine must work together or the machine breaks down. I sometimes feel that if I lost a finger I should have to amputate myself.

Now that these things have been restored and the mayor's house takes the tangle out of problems, I have been deciding not to make a difficulty about the nightingale and the wastepaper basket. Keats, who was racked by the critics in his need to share his universe, made a mistake about this piece. Perhaps he thought it did not 'say anything', it was not a 'great work' such as *Hyperion* and

Endymion were supposed to be. Writers are their own worst critics not in their harshness but in their blindness where their own work is concerned.

I am always rather suspicious of this business of saying something, because art at its highest form speaks but does not need to transmit messages. It may or it may not, but they are no criterion. Many of the greatest writers have ardent messages, but it is not that which makes them writers in themselves. And who but himself would accuse Keats, blind in embalmed darkness, of saying nothing to the world? Among 'the murmurous haunt of flies on summer eves' he made a picture through the sense of smell as accurate as a photographer's, and that sufficed.

'Even a cabbage is worth writing about if the writing is good,' a friend of mine asserted in a bout of indignation over a travel book which she claimed to be devoid of style or purpose. I do not know why the poor cabbage has become the scapegoat for all that is placid and uninteresting. I am rather fond of cabbages myself and think them quite as good-looking as many other vegetables.

Its own misuse is a good example of the misuse of words. 'Ugh, cabbage!' with a sneer means 'institutional cabbage that is watery and cooked to tastelessness with the possibility of being not one hundred per cent vegetable,' whereas 'cabbage' in the Greek autumn means that summer is ending and the longed-for rain has come, the land is turning green, the farmers are singing and busy and — crunch — after months of dedication to tomato salad, the almost white, the light green-yellow cabbage with copious oil and lemon indulges our forgotten tendencies to be rabbits. I shall record a cabbage, I now have a strong urge to make a picture of this line of cabbages which is my last sight before the hot siesta, blowing with outstretched sails of leaves among its more highly respected companions in the orchard, indicating the force of the north wind, and gleaming about its shadowed veins with all the colours seen in the variable light of olive groves.

Photography, among the lesser of the arts, is yet the epitome of all. Where it records with beauty it is articulate, it is 'the world in a grain of sand' which a child knows, a statement of the truth.

In the 'Ode to a Nightingale' we ask for nothing else, yet if Keats really felt it necessary to be 'saying something' he might still have let it pass. Or perhaps he did not realise that he was putting on record a running commentary of the activities of his Muse. He told us a great deal about her.

Can I in this day and age say 'she'? Calliope, Terpsichore and all that troupe are difficult to sort out or deal with, partly because the branches of the arts do overlap inextricably, and if one could remember all their names it would still be next to impossible to remember exactly who is in charge of what. Perhaps that is why they have been taken to be female — it is in the nature of their work that they should be elusive and provoking. They also have the power to destroy.

Gerard Manley Hopkins, who mistook his muse for God, was tortured by one of the most sensitive conflicts for which they have been responsible. How could he live as man or priest or poet when all his different parts were perpetually at loggerheads, when his universe was splintered and the pieces of his wholeness did not fit? Poetry and his Jesuit calling were antagonists.

> ... *pitched past pitch of grief*
> *More pangs will, schooled at forepangs, wilder wring.*

God and the devil must sometimes have seemed to be masquerading in each other's suits. One or the other, the muse or typhus fever broke him, and no one can know which was which, but there is no doubt that the muse had her influence.

Because of her, or whatever we are to call her, whoever is more a writer than anything else is a writer; whoever is more a sculptor is a sculptor; an alpha artist is an alpha artist, a gamma artist gamma but an artist, and failure to be so is a sin. For writers, said the gods, must write, and painters paint, sculptors must sculpt, they said, musicians compose; so it was decreed from the beginning, this is the law. The artist pledges himself very early, with a painting or a poem at five years, to some direction to which he is already committed by his birth, and then there is nothing much that he can do about it, circumstances, which are his subconscious servants, take over, but he is a servant too — as long as he is whole.

I used to malign the muse by thinking, 'I want to write, but I don't know what to write about,' not realising that each muse is integrated with her art and does not function by herself. The world, one might for instance say, has been explored, and though we are all travellers in a sense from birth to death there is little scope remaining for purely factual travelogue. Not only that, our very language has been explored as well. Those of us who try to write have been preceded by a hundred masters of the first degree, several thousands of the lower orders, and sometimes when I write a phrase which pleases me, especially one which comes easily as if I knew it, I think, 'Is this my own? Did I write this, or did I read it once?'

All this might be said, and so an American who lives and writes in Freya's Italian neighbourhood complained to me by her fireside one evening until he grew so intense about the matter that he asserted that language was worn out. Somehow or other a replacement must be found. And what did he suggest? In the face of female attack he simply stuck to his ideal without solution, the English language is over-used to death, words must be replaced by something else.

Freya, who had been sitting quietly with her embroidery, said, somewhat severely and with complete conviction, 'There is nothing less used than the English language.'

Here is the final stage of liberation. If this is so the way is open and the English language, badly treated, is waiting to be used. Add to this her observation in an essay, 'More and more as I see it the travel book is becoming an interpretation', and we are given all the scope we want for cabbages.

Interpretation, like poetry, is bound to be a personal affair, and I do not think that one can make it without being entirely self-centred unless one has some sort of relation with a recipient. If poetry, as the most personal form of expression, is the result of various sensitive people letting their emotions overflow about the world, we accuse all poets of being egoists and the world of being scavengers. Both accusations are avoidable. Artists are not necessarily exceptional, nor different from others in anything but their method of expression, nor are they outsiders. Each is a possessor of the universe, each a part of the history of the world, and the readers, listeners, spectators, in recognising that history in themselves, themselves in that history, are almost equally the artist and must be allowed the opportunity to be so, for all that they lack is that they receive what they receive at second hand.

But at the moment of creation whom does the artist bear in mind? Does he think of strangers or of friends? I do not know, but I know that all statues have wings, some of stately pendelic marble, others of stone from lesser quarries, but they were made to fly. I know that an actor, while he is performing, cannot see into the dark beyond the footlights, yet that darkness is no void. 'Did you have a good audience tonight?' What should that matter to the quality of his performance? The good audience helps the actor, for its members are part of what is happening in the theatre, and it is the personal link with those unseen, unknown faces which completes in the artist what the unseen muse begins.

CHAPTER TEN

Jason and the Virgin

AIYIÁLI is becoming daily more absorbing and the way up to Langátha urgent. It is August, the Virgin Mary's month and the people of the village are guardians of her festival. The Feast of the Assumption as celebrated remotely in the mountains, and later in the day in our *platía*, is cheerful and obscure. Nothing here can vie with the pomp, the confusion and the crowds of Tinos or disrupt the shipping timetables with an overflow of pilgrims who are not island-born, yet we have a small upheaval in our life.

Grazing in the country thirty or more goats are doomed. Yorgo's mother, as well as sewing for the village, is sewing new suits for her own boys, grey and white checks for all three, shorts for the little ones. The summer influx of relations keeps the *platía* awake to later hours and there are twenty or thirty people at midday on the beach. Boats come pounding in, sickened by the meltemi which blew throughout July and, knowing that we are sheltered, has learnt to curl and swoop. Families converge to meet their 'own people' from the mainland and their sons from cargo boats around the world. Blow out, wind, and die, for next week I shall be on reception too. My brother and his wife whom I have not seen for over three years are coming with Jason, their six-month-old adopted son. My well is almost dry — will nappies be combustible? Costa comes regularly with water and pours it out around the lemon trees. I want perfection, I want still, August heat. I must buy candles. Food will be forthcoming. I must get Costa to bring me a camp bed.

As I worked on a tight schedule of lessons to ease the first days of this visit my piles of notes became increasingly domestic, and gave way entirely to absorption in household beauty, bedclothes and the number of mules that would be needed for an efficient reception on the quay. On the morning of the seventh Yorgo arrived for his English lesson with an eagerness to be the one to bring up my brother's family that night, and for the next fortnight I made no attempt at work at all.

The boy looked disappointed when I said that I had already ordered two mules and so was I. Nobody thought that I could back out of my arrangement, but the honour of Aiyiáli, which irked a little at that moment, was the pleasure of the following fortnight, and I could always call on Yorgo at the end.

My relations would have had to be excessively rude and ugly not to be admired, and however much anyone may have regarded them as the beginning of a tourist movement Henry, Catherine and Jason were received first and foremost as people, as individuals, and my own status rose and remains higher since I was able to produce a family in flesh and blood. For a few days before their much-spoken-of arrival my way through the village was lined with a chorus of new greetings, '*Kaló dhéximo!* Good receiving!' and when they came, '*Kaló dhéximo!*' with handshakes, but still largely for myself; the strangers were not to be overwhelmed with careless familiarity at first. Families really are of paramount importance; I am sure that my responses were appropriate. *Kaló dhéximo!* It felt like Easter Day.

I woke the first morning of their visit on a camp bed on the balcony to see Costa watering the lemon trees below. The day before I had drawn the last muddy residue out of the well, had not had time to deal with what suddenly became a top-priority emergency, and now was agonised to see that precious liquid disappear into the earth. We did not start the day with a tour of village architecture, we started it with a concerted hunt for water and a nappy washer.

The latter was to be discovered among the lower houses, for where there is no washerwoman one has only to consider who

E

has a good well; the second woman whom I asked agreed. Our only problem was how to fix a price, so much a day, but what would 'so much' be? 'What do you think?' she asked me.

'I don't know. What do you say?'

'I've no idea, I'll ask the teacher. Give me the clothes and we won't quarrel,' she said. 'We won't quarrel' is the Greek answer to every indecisive bill, but it is not satisfactory for sometimes one does feel like quarrelling afterwards. Every day she was to take the clothes, and every day to put the onus on me, and we continued to prevaricate, deferring the certain moment of embarrassment.

This woman's well was deep in water, but it was near home that we had to find a daily bucketful. Towards the middle of the morning in a heatwave we had made sure of water rights, and then discovered, in our own house, cool in the old kitchen, four huge cans which Costa had brought up and left for us. Figs, grapes, tomatoes, cost no one more than natural thoughtfulness, shamefully we had to throw out the surplus every day, but the gift of water is manna in the wilderness, the gift of water should canonise a saint.

Our first arrival on the beach was greeted with reticence and coffee and subsequent arrivals with such pleasure on all sides that I have realised a new ambition for my situation on the island, to teach without receiving money, exchange without reckoning. But for Sophia's mother I would have no access when I am alone to roast pigeon, cream cheese, spinach pies. But for the accumulation of all the parents' feeling of responsibility towards me as their children's teacher, this fortnight would never have passed so happily. I saw my own people honoured and all those mothers had the best excuse for indulging their inveterate quality of baby love. Jason was adored.

Greek peasants with their donkeys are rather like Americans with their cars, and Greek peasant babies are almost never seen except bleached in the confines of their homes. Our behaviour in walking daily to the beach with all our paraphernalia and a baby on our back, with a white muslin sun-shade halo-like above his head, would have been certifiable if we had not been so good. One wayside scene when he grew hungry nearly asphyxiated a farmer with hysteria. Henry put the baby on his knee and did the bottle work himself. 'The father!' hiccoughed the farmer lurching on his mule. Jason, who obviously thrived on walks and beaches, who was guaranteed to enrapture everyone with smiles the moment that we placed him in the intriguing backpack, was very soon the best-known baby in Aiyiáli, and now that he has gone, 'Where is Jason?' the village and the harbour call, not 'Where's the baby?' and, 'Have you heard from Jason yet?' It was characteristic of these people that they coddled little over him and gave him, properly, the status of a person.

New eyes bring new revelations. In spite of all indebtedness from some, the characters who in the end brought most delight were those who owed me nothing. Costa was one, but he hardly made his presence known except by those valuable water-cans which he continued to deposit, for the best part of a week. Stephanáki, the violin-playing cobbler, became Catherine's favourite within the first two days. Until he told me his life's history, three-quarter's of which concerns the bench where he is now at work, I did not know his age and could not guess, for his tufty hair is sixty-year-old grey, and his black eyes are teenage bright. Forty-two, I think, is the correct medium; he is the twinkling cobbler of a fairy tale and has been as near as one can be a helpful trial to me ever since I came to Amorgós. His shop is always shut when I am most in need; he nearly sent me off to Astypálaia barefoot when he kept my sandals by him for three days and developed a mental block against donating each two nails. Even so I shall eventually have accumulated a summer's lessons' worth when his daughter reaches the foreign-language age; it just happens that my sandals invariably collapse before a journey, and invariably this is the moment when he is feeling musical.

Henry and Catherine wanted sandals, and it was a week before the festival of the Virgin Mary which ranks in our village on the scale of Easter Day. Stephanáki blinked. 'You want them before the Panayía?'

'Sooner, if you can. And they want them just like mine.'
Stephanáki looked melancholy. 'You need a strap behind.'

He had a bunch of paper cuttings, with straps behind, around and over, straps of every dimension except on the Mykoniot pattern like my own. When we had admired and rejected all the possibilities and when his oratory on all the advantages of all his own and all the disadvantages of mine had failed, he drew breath by reverting to his former question, 'Do you want them soon?'

He had not made such sandals. That was his worry. He is a craftsman and he feared the possibility of making a mistake. However, since we were adamant, he capitulated and informed me that he would keep my own to copy.

I was rather glad. Rough ways make the soles of feet tough and destroy the soles of shoes, so I can see no reason for the latter during summer except on hillsides where the heads of gorse bushes cling on like miniature sea urchins, or when the sand is burning. Island convention is all that makes me wear shoes, but since Stephanáki was forcing me to jettison convention I could freely be a goat. Considering how long he had taken over hammering four nails before, I would doubtless end the fortnight with fine hooves.

But the cobbler is not lazy, he is Greek. The Greeks do nothing or everything at once. Within thirty-six hours he had called at our house in person for a fitting and enjoyed two or three pieces of flapjack made in Gussage All Saints by my mother and tenderly transported with an equally unprecedented bag of gooseberries by air. This was probably the zenith of my achievement on the island, when Stephanáki knelt munching my mother's handwork at my brother's feet. I decided to send back *halvá* and almonds in return. They would be sure to please.

Then he became absorbed. Once he discovered that he could achieve what had been ordered he began to work with love. Only on one occasion Henry and Catherine discovered a musical session in his shop, and then he admitted them with some betrayal of guilt, not understanding that they came in because they liked to hear. Otherwise he worked as if he had no other order, no rival occupation, nothing else to create before the Panayía, and probably infuriated his other customers. The soles of these new sandals were not nailed but sewn on; they were ready in three days. And then he looked at them and smiled, and smiled whenever he saw them walking in the street. 'On the night of the Panayía,' he told me sternly, 'you will come and sit by me.'

But before anything else happened I had to work out this business of the nappy washing which went on every day. Only a fifty-drachma note 'to be getting on with' had changed hands and I suspected that, prompted by the teacher, the woman had decided in a hopeful way that it might cover one day's work alone. 'Never mind,' she said when I suggested that this was overdoing things, 'Don't give me any more. I'll go on with the washing and when your brother leaves you can give English lessons to my boy.' I had become so island minded that I very nearly wavered and agreed.

Catherine pointed out that this would be carrying auntliness a little far, and encouraged me to let them spend their dollars generously. The predicament, even concerning baby clothes, was not trivial since I was forced to sacrifice either the washerwoman's hope or the balance of the island's standard of finance. Mean as I felt at the time I am glad I chose the first.

'But this is Amorgós,' they laugh when I tell them of the fees for English lessons in the capital, and we quickly reduce the quoted sum to a fifth plus a few grapes. I think it tremendously important to the stability of such a place to keep it stable, to let it move upward steadily but not to bombshell it with notes. So I made a pompous speech of which the outcome was that I would give her five drachmas less a bundle than for a top-price English lesson and have some onions please. She looked a little disappointed but did not complain, and I will go on buying onions from her.

'We really are serious about a plot of land,' said Henry.

The statement, which I suppose had been begun when I embezzled his funds two years ago, sounded among the washing like another of the domestic pleasures of the day. Their journey, which was a fortnight cut out of a holiday in England, a journey not to Greece but Amorgós — they did not even take a detour into

Athens between the airport and Piraeus — had seemed dynamic from the first, but the dynamo was working so well and naturally that we just smiled and said, 'Well then, let's buy some land.'

But for their own exactitude the whole business might have been done and finished with inside a day. As soon as they decided that they wanted land above the beach on the sheltered curl of the far end of the bay we had only to go into the orchard underneath to find one-legged Anápyros, the owner, watering his bean crop, and he with great agility navigated walls and paths and minor landslides to display what he would sell. It was not out of character that Henry chose the cheapest area from preference, this being the highest, most rugged, and most difficult for mules. 'If this land is going to be developed,' he said, 'I want to be on top.' At the moment the hillside has one house.

The next day Anápyros' brother-in-law Spiro, a builder, whom he was obviously promoting, came up with us to measure off twenty square metres of the land, and Anápyros began to talk about a contract and could not understand why Henry wanted time. He spent hours on the rock surveying, and all the inhabitants of the orchards watched in curiosity while this figure moved about for hours through the afternoon and into semi-darkness for two days, when all felt that the site could be put down on paper and signed off right away. 'He's an architect, you see,' I said, 'he understands much better than we do,' and everyone was impressed until he came down to confront Anápyros with a plan in in which the size had doubled and every side was a different measurement.

The butterflies, settling and resettling under the leaves of the fig tree where we sheltered, are the butterflies of a fairy tale, continuously enacting a transformation scene. Flying they are scarlet, and as they close to rest they change their shape and colour, but you cannot see it happen — suddenly they have folded up their wings to arrow heads and are jet black. Look, the leaves and trunk are covered with bat-like triangles — shake, and there is a scarlet flutter through the shade.

'But how many square metres?' Anápyros demanded. 'What is

the length and breadth? Didn't you measure the plot with Spiro, twenty metres square? How can the scribe write down what you have here?'

A mountainside, we said, is irregular. It is not square.

But what is the length and breadth?

I think I should say 'clerk' instead of 'scribe', but the word *grammatikós* suggests the latter, he is 'the grammared one' and that is really his position in Langátha. A small, stern man with a smooth parchment face, he smiles and relents only during his musical sessions in Stephanáki's shop when he plays the bouzouki in duet. He intimidates me, I have never received a smile from him myself. He and the president, who has the quayside grocery, are the two people qualified to make a pseudo contract in the absence of the *symvoliográphos*, the contract writer 'who may come one day'. The paper that we must make, we were assured, would have no legal value whatsoever, but anyway, said Anápyros, why spend a thousand drachmas on a piece of paper when the scribe can write one for nothing very well?

Meanwhile he would sign nothing until Henry had cleared up his metres to something which he could comprehend and the rock been tamed, with a certain latitude, to squares. The plot enlarged again and gained considerably from the uphill measurement. Finally, on 14 August, all were satisfied, and Anápyros had the brilliant idea that the best time to make the so-called contract would be at midday on the morrow when everyone concerned was bound to be converging in Langátha on the way home from the church.

The village was bulging to its peak capacity, which is not large but tight. Caïques arrived from Katápola and Captain Dimitri stepped off with his violin. Stephanáki had begun feeling musical long before the appointed time, and the doodle painters persevered and won a temporary victory over the donkeys and the mules. In the evening we went out into the country to the Panayía. We should have been there in the afternoon eating a fasting mess of barley with the populace, but I knew that there was something better at an unofficial hour to be seen.

Now for a moment, at ten o'clock without a moon, feeling the obscure way through rocks and fields and mountainside with a baby sleeping in his carry cot, my words seemed doubtful, my promise grew improbable. There will be, I told them, a ruined house beside a church with stars and vines dangling above your heads, with thirty or forty carcasses of goats, perhaps a cow or two, and thirty or forty people being cooks and butchers around two long marble tables, chopping by the light of lamp and fire where the meat is being braised. It seemed unlikely in this waste of dark and silence, and it all proved true.

Costa was standing in the doorway and welcomed us, leading us into the inner regions to choose the anatomy of the meal which he assumed that we must want, deciding on a heap of tongue. I do not know why goat should be despised. It does not mince, the president informed me when I wanted to make spaghetti sauce and he had nothing else, but the beast well cooked is difficult to tell from lamb, which — I am also told — gives rheumatism while goat does not. Certainly these tongues were among the most tender and delicious meats that I have eaten. We set them down with a flagon of retsina among the women shredding garlic into outsize bowls of island earthenware, and while we ate the braiser stood over his cauldron in a gondolier pose, leaning forward on his five-foot oar.

The hackers and the shredders loved an audience. 'Give us work,' we said and joined the second group ourselves. Jason woke to smile on the procedure for ten minutes and earn us all our goats' tongues for the pleasure which he gave while we ingrained our hands with garlic juice, and went to sleep again. We moved him outside, away from the appreciative noise.

A long-moustached old farmer, Marki, notoriously drunk on each day of the year except those four when he cooks for festivals, crouched over an open fire bubbling the workers' supper which smelt remarkably appetising for a fasting eve. Costa leant against the wall and began to talk about cement. Would he, Henry asked, help him flag the land? Henry had been moved towards him from the moment when he had appeared a day or two before at the window of my overflowing orchard cottage which looks out on his field, and handed Catherine a bunch of grapes. It was not the gesture which had impressed, for it is difficult at this time of year to go anywhere without receiving grapes, it was their quality. They were large and sumptuous black like those one gives as an extravagance to invalids in hospital, and Henry immediately felt that anyone who could raise such bunches so near such pippy ones as were growing in similar circumstances on both sides could be relied upon in any of his working roles.

Costa is the backbone of a country Greek community, the sort of man who would drive a trade union off its head. He has mules and other animals, he has a boat, a beach and fields, he appears at all places and all times unassumingly and energetically, and can provide at any moment any article or utensil required for any constructive, agricultural or domestic purpose, and any piece of information if it is practical, but like Langátha he is practical with doodles.

Certainly he would help us place the corner posts. Tomorrow was the festival, but he guaranteed to wake us early the next morning, for it did not seem unreasonable to suppose that his working day would be unaffected by a night of dance. Cement, mules, metal posts, all these could be arranged, and now the long moustache pronounced his cooking ready and we were bidden join the working party at the marble table once again. The only trouble about this rich herbiferous stew was that it formed our second supper on the eve of the official feast. Well, never mind, if we were stymied at the public meal nothing would taste so good or look so beautiful as at this mad, flickering midnight hour while we waited for the moon to rise and help us home.

It poured with rain. On 15 August in the middle of the Aegean, at midday, a storm swept up, doors, windows crashed and rain came pelting down. I wish I could have witnessed, from a distance, the scene on Tinos where twenty thousand pilgrims is the annual norm. We had done our duty, dressed up ourselves and Jason, lit our candles, presented him to the happiest man of the day, our village priest, had done our best with soup and meat, and were heavily returning to the village when everyone's best clothes were drenched. Anápyros' sense of timing seemed particularly inapt. Of course all the people required to make a contract were gathering; a siesta was their only need. 'The afternoon...' we said.

Anápyros turned out to be the husband of the *cafenion* keeper who is Stephanáki's female counterpart in twinkling, and who gives me herbs and the free run of her fig trees because 'you buy your cigarettes from me, don't you?' which is accommodating of her when hers is the only shop with a tobacco licence in my neighbourhood. This large, high-beamed, wooden-floored interior was the scene which we tried to make into a meeting place with the formidable scribe, but when he did come in the afternoon it was only to reproach Anápyros for choosing to do business on the Virgin Mary's Day. He was so busy being severe that he could hear no question as to when he might make himself available, and shortly afterwards was seated with his bouzouki beside Stephanáki for a celebration that was likely to last into the following day.

The night was fine. Apart from the Virgin's midday storm my hopes of August were consistently surpassed. In obedience to the cobbler we sat as close to his group as we could, and that, in the crush of the *platía*, is very close. If any musician on this night wants to be appreciated by a chosen audience it must be so, for the rival instruments and the rival songs run into one another at three or four metres' distance among the tables and the dance, and all is one indistinguishable wail. From the house we recognised the most persistent, the most piercing sound, as Stephanáki's song. All the singing of every musician — and there were two dozen gathered there — seemed as it struck our doors to be issuing from Stephanáki's mouth. We felt that we had been living with it for all times.

We had had our festival the night before, and working on a baby-sitting rota went home as soon as we had sent the bottles that were due from us around several other tables and dealt as best we could with those that kept appearing on our own. We slept, and woke again in daylight to Stephanáki's wail. The general hubbub had subsided and I could hear debate among the last group of survivors about going home, a suggestion always broken into by a new bout of song. What seemed like the last stages of the night at six o'clock revived at seven, at eight was going strong, and by this time Costa, after two hours' sleep, was busy in the courtyard watering the lemons and cutting down the apple tree.

I cried out, seeing his work lay stark the railings along the balcony, but it was dying and destructive, and I submerged my protests in talk about our land. He would be down on the shore the whole of the next day, he promised, and at any time that Henry came would leave his work and go with him to plant the posts. But the contract, official or not, must be on paper first. 'You must be firm with Anápyros, Carolina, you must go to him now and say, "The contract must be made today."' A next-to-last gasp of bouzouki wavered into the courtyard. 'That's the scribe with Stephanáki,' Costa said. 'Go now.'

One has to feel brave at any hour to confront the scribe. I felt more than usually brave as I dressed to confront him after a musical night which was still being fairly musical at nine o'clock. 'When can you make the contract for this plot of land? Do you think you will wake up in the afternoon?' The words hardly seemed appropriate.

The last survivors had moved inside Anápyros' *magazí*, and I must give credit to the scribe for the greatest stamina of all the musicians of the night. He was as spruce as always and as self-composed, while beside him Stephanáki was betraying the greatest difficulty in keeping his rolling head in place. The only exercise by which he could achieve this was to squeeze out the death-throes of the night's song with the agony with which the sambouna or the bagpipes scream out if accidentally pressed. Pause and wobble, Stephanáki, squeeze your lungs again.

I accepted a tumblerful of light retsina while the scribe rested his feet on the rungs of my chair and was almost affable. 'When you come up from the harbour — don't you come up at seven or eight? — we'll make the contract then.'

The date seemed likely to lead us into hours of waiting, but it was then, when we arrived unhurriedly, that this unlikely winner of the endurance test impressed us most. At half-past seven he was standing in the *platía* waiting, the paper was already written out and only to be signed. He had slept, he said, two hours, and seemed to thrive on such a day; he may always be efficient but I have never known him be so cordial. Two thousand drachmas were passed across the table, the rest would be sent at once in my name from the States. 'If it is late in coming you can keep Carolina as a hostage,' Henry said.

Kaló ríziko! Good rooting! It took Henry and Costa two and a half hot morning hours to root those metal posts securely in the corners of the rocky plot, and when they came down sweating at midday I ran to meet them with a bottle of cold beer. They had had no need of me before; a few words in common and much sympathy sufficed. Now we sank into the shade of Anápyros' fig trees among the butterflies, and all that could be achieved this summer had been done. Do you have beer in England, asked Anápyros. How much does it cost? What do you make it of? What other fruit do you produce? Does England have coal? And steel? And what else? Why has the pound fallen? Is Mr Wilson a good man?

Costa came to supper with us in the evening, the last before my people left. Let's get the business of money over quickly, we agreed; how much did we owe? Expenses, he said, were fifty drachmas, and that would do. As for the labour, that was nothing, he and the mules had been there anyway. Henry, who had needed a substantial siesta afterwards and had been somewhat irked to see from the cottage window how Costa went straight on working in the field, insisted that the labour had its worth. He asked about the sand for making cement blocks, for obviously the reason why so many new Greek houses disintegrate so quickly as they do is that the sand is taken straight from beaches full of salt. Henry wanted a deposit made on his plot in the winter to be washed out by the rain.

'I can let you have sand,' said Costa, 'for a drachma a bucket, but it's poor quality. They say there may be a mechanical sand-grinder next year, and that would be the best and cheapest, but it's not certain yet. You might do well to wait. The second best and most expensive is the sand I bring by boat. But that is three and a half drachma for a bucketful.'

As Costa lacks the cunning to cheat, so he lacks it consciously to impress; the architect, however, was impressed. 'Then will you deliver me a thousand buckets of your best sand?' he said. We agreed that the grinder was as airy as our road. 'By next year the salt should be washed out, but could you build some bricks around it so that we won't lose any in the wind?'

'Bah!' said Costa, 'if you put bricks up there they will be stolen. People will come down from Thollária. Leave it to me, I have my methods. Besides, it's my responsibility, if any sand is lost the loss is mine. Order a thousand buckets, you will come back and find a thousand buckets. If you like I'll measure them.'

We were all in difficulties over our spaghetti which was of the thickest variety and determined to be comical. Henry brought in and lighted our last candle and conversation turned to Greek dialects and from there to English accents and to Welsh. 'Greek is more like English,' I told Costa, 'than Welsh is. And there's a little village, about the size of this one, called Llanfairpwllgwyn-wyllgogerychchwyrndrobwllllantysiliogogogoch.'

Costa looked bemused. 'Tell him,' said Henry, 'that it's as long as the whole platform when you come in by train.'

Then Costa, the plain, blunt jack of all trades, and master of most of them if little else, looked up and said, 'Perhaps it is as long as a rainbow?'

CHAPTER ELEVEN

Stroumbo and the Animals

THE sun was rising as I left the harbour, and I walked into Langátha in broad daylight. The midnight boat on which Henry and Catherine left had come in at five o'clock when Jason was beginning to think it time for a new day and they were sated with the last. I sat down on the way up outside Vassili's shop and received from his wife condolences for which she seemed much in need herself. Vassili too, who had carried polite restraint so far at first that Henry had felt him to be surly, had nearly wept over the leave-taking which was completed with that most generous of summer gifts, four eggs. 'Anyway, Carolina,' they said sensibly, 'now you can get back to work. I don't suppose you have done much since they came.' How true. I felt tired. What great thoughts were with me now? The best thing to do with houses is to live in them. The mayor's house had not been so lived in for ten years.

Shall I leave on 14 September? There is only a boat to Syra once a week, from which I shall go to Mykonos. I shall leave on the fourteenth, though it is the feast of Stavrós, the Holy Cross. I do not need another festival. And so I have a fortnight in which to deal with all these notes entitled Stroumbo, the deserted village of the well-toothed centenarian which in the spring I took as the obvious symbol of a dying world.

Where, I would say, are the descendants of the Stroumbots in their multiplicity? They have overflowed into the overweighted places to weigh them down again, to swamp the hot Athenian pavements, cover suburban hills with bungalows and, as drivers, not understand the meaning of white lines. Where are the Stroumbots? I would write a chapter about that.

I am doing my best, and I believe what I am saying, and yet Aiyiáli, which points out these things clearly, defies at the same time the prolonged harangue. And what do you know, it says, about population trends?

Mrs Gandhi, I would answer on the mule track, is preaching three children followed by sterilisation and a transistor, and that is sensible, and the British Government increases the family allowance for the fourth child, which would be sensible if the country were under-populated. Why not instead reinstate the poll tax? Why not be really hard-headed and double the tax on children of retarded parents, children who are . . . no. Such far-fetched ideas arise to be rejected sadly, and then I think, we have put ourselves into such a predicament as can only be solved by some far-fetchedness.

How then, I wondered, was I to say without presumption that the world is on the verge of a catastrophe equal to the seven plagues? We have grown so clever in this century, competing with the laws of nature, vying with her on her own ground, straining her patience and resources that sooner or later she will assert her rights and as a matter of necessity, if we don't blow ourselves up first, will put us in collision with another planet or produce another flood. See, you silly people, the universe will laugh, you were not gods.

I came here prepared with statistics about planets, stars and meteorites, my notes tell me of several Bible sources from which I might have cribbed. I had learnt how horrific miracles could be put into scientific terms and how the full force of their reality could be repeated once again, though since we — and I can scarcely credit it — belong to the milky way it may it not be of great significance. I was prepared for speeches, I still believe the subject of the speech, but it had seemed to be too solemn to set down without stirring language, the prophetic and the Biblical, and that has been forbidden here. Aiyiáli dictates, the mule track tells me, 'Everything may be as bad as you had thought it, say so then and drop the oratory.' The way has been didactic all the summer — put in this and exclude that and do not pretend to be an astrologer.

The best thing to be said about the stars is that they are beautiful. During the few days of summer when I cannot sleep indoors their shining is as distracting as the heat. They are more distracting than attracting; that, as I see it, is their proper purpose, they are conducive to creative thinking because they empty the mind and allow room for ideas to swim. I think that everyone ought to have two or three star nights a year and otherwise leave them to themselves.

When Peggy Glanville Hicks told me in Athens of her father's comment on God and the world, how he lacked experience and went on to do better in other realms, I really thought that I could quote from him and make *An Early Work* the title of a book, but while I sit and think of that there is always something about this island to deter. 'The children are leaving,' an old woman muttered as she passed me on her donkey, 'and Langátha will be Stroumbo soon,' and I know that, much as I commend its way of living, that way relies on the support of working sons abroad. And yet as I write I hear the turning of wet cement on spades in the school playground, a pleasant sound when agitated by manpower alone, asserting that Stroumbo is not by necessity our fate. Anápyros is building a new shop in the *platía*, houses fall and houses are restored. Langátha, which places so much hope in the outside, yet gives hope to those of us who come, and as long as it survives forbids the writing of *An Early Work*. Heaven help my readers if it dies.

'Now you are a landowner, and will have a house here of your own.'

'It's my brother's land, not mine.'

'Well that's the same thing, isn't it?'

Family feeling is certainly to be a boon to me, and yet Henry and Catherine, tying me more closely to the island, have also reestablished a link with the outside, a place which is apparently one great delirium. 'We could not be surprised by Bobby Kennedy's assassination,' Catherine said. But that is a terrible thing that you are saying. What are you telling me about the world?

'The Greeks are in a deep sleep,' a malcontent in Athens told me, 'it is bad.' Oh, but I think, however uncharacteristic their post-revolution mood, there may be a good deal to be said for somnolence today. So the junta frightened off a few thousand foreigners? It frightened them from one country in the world where there is, generally speaking, *isichía*, peace and quiet, peacefulness. 'Yes,' said my friend, 'but this is compulsory *isichía*.'

Compulsory *isichía*! The United States is in a ferment. Washington is burning. Paris is prostrated, and all the too-many people who have left their Stroumbos empty are angry people too. Democratic or undemocratic, I can see an argument for a little compulsory *isichía* somewhere if it is not permanent.

What happened last night on the quayside to disturb the harbour's *isichía*? Skinny old Adoni — who else he is but that I do not know — began to dance with me, and quickly he evolved a shooting symbol which turned our exhibition to a hunting scene and thereafter, since I was wearing a red shirt, into a bullfight, and thus we passed the time of all those waiting for the boat. Thank the gods for Greek spontaneity.

While Adoni adapted himself to my energetic ignorance and we indulged in mutual madnesses outside, two young girls — Athenian cousins of sixteen and twelve, half islanders by birth — were practising the *hassápiko* indoors. The performance is far more skilled and far more creditable, and the *hassápiko* is assured another lease of life.

Did I say that I would not dance this year? How we deceive ourselves. 'Stay down this evening,' they call along the quayside, 'and make us laugh again.' Gladly I will — next year. But what happened that evening that I burst out of my Amorgós restraint? September has begun. The villagers have lit their bonfires in honour of 31 August. Burn away the summer, sing through the streets, only so far do we abandon *isichía*. Dance the bullfight on the quay, September presages the autumn, and the restlessness has come.

I lie on the mayor's great iron bedstead and consider a new feature in the room. There are wooden curtain rails here, crowned centrally in diamond shape, strong to bear the weight of winter curtains for those long evenings when the family inhabiting these quarters warmed each other by proximity and the charcoal brazier. There should not be a winter for communities that have no proper heating, it offends their natural nobility. The family are seldom washed except for face and hands, or do the maids bring up hot water in great cauldrons from the cookhouse underneath? Not in excess. Now the old aristocrat, whose taste, like the Georgians', was good and solid, comes toppling down for a moment in my estimation; slightly indisposed he rises to go out on to that balcony, down the slithery staircase, and blast his way through the back garden in the rain. The whitewashed hole among the outhouses is a summer pleasure. Even the mayor has human weaknesses.

I have felt so natural, so unselfconscious through the summer, it is a shock to wake up in the middle of the night and find that I am thinking, 'If I drive from Istanbul to Padua I must have dollars for emergencies,' or wondering how the vine and the mulberry are protecting my tyres in Panagítsa. September has come in with alien thoughts and I am growing alien as well.

'Stay for the winter,' they say, 'since you like our island.'

'Not on your life.'

'Stay for the winter, it is beautiful.' But I am a part of all that I have met, and all the other parts wait in their time to be reclaimed. To stay here any longer than two weeks would be to turn my existence here into a lie. '*Marídhes!* Whitebait!' shout the fishermen. '*Ephimerídhes!* Newspapers!' is the cry of Athens. *Marídhes! Ephimerídhes!* There is a long way to go.

Will there be elections in Greece as promised by the colonels? Elections are interesting again. Longer than a fortnight is too long. So what is happening out there in that mad world? What is what country called? Where do we have riots? What kings are on what thrones? Longer is too long. I have not the stamina of the islanders for so much *isichía* for years on end. I came here to look at the world, not to escape. I shall go and drink vodka on the Bosphorus and I shall say, Aiyiáli this, Aiyiáli that, and even be nostalgic, but four days was the limit of my endurance here in April, two and a half months is perfect for the summer, and admiring the islanders I know that — for myself — to develop the guts to live it longer would be to take a backward turn. I am in no way disillusioned — I do not think I have illusions. I like the island just as much.

Is it possible to retain that awareness of things which one acquires in the place where the smallest detail has a value of its own? I would like that to be my gain when I go out. Such islands are not the place for lotus eating, but rather for the growth of sensitivity. It is the large-scale emotion that numbs. In England we turn on, say, the television, and a Romanian girl is competing in the Olympic women's ice dancing championships for her country, at eleven years old. The beauty of this ethereal accomplishment flashes before her international audience in a performance which I must believe because I see it with my own eyes. Then, while we are still strung up on the height of fantasy we are confronted with a Vietnamese girl of about the same age blocking her ears against the gunfire in which she has been separated from her parents, and we are scraped against the floor of human suffering.

What are we to do about this volley-ball treatment of our emotions in which each triumph and each downfall contains some ingredient which is the world's and so our own? Seeing such pictures I think sometimes that we should lament with all the downcast of the world and rejoice with all the elated. It is too much to demand, we are forced into a middle channel, but it should be possible.

Perhaps it is because of our inability to bounce continually between the heights and depths that our reactions are so inadequate. Riots and nervous disorders shake our homes and countries while centuries of history are casually thrust aside, and the uproar in the end is over whether or not the healthy adult worker should pay half a crown for his own medicine, or the suing of a cigarette company because someone has developed lung cancer from its cigarettes. Mad world, I cannot understand your sense of balance. The rhyme and the reason.... The purpose and the balance.... I am heading back to Julia and the Phengári now.

I shall go there, and I shall use its napkins, but I think that I may put them to a better use.

I have learnt about awareness, and I know why Jason seems more important than the seven plagues. As far as I am concerned he is. The festival of the Virgin Mary and a plot of land became my life, and while one should not turn a blind eye to enormities, and while there are many more too many people in the world today than when I came to Amorgós two months ago, all the teaching of the mule track has boiled down into one of the earliest proverbs of childhood concerning pounds and pence. How can I be so commonplace? I can always do more tinkering. 'Be chic among pence' — it amounts to the same — 'and the pounds will be chic by themselves.'

The commonplace at all events is interesting and intricate. I like deciding, if I have ten drachmas, between a bus and lunch. I like, if I have a hundred, to spend seventy on a taxi into Athens from an island boat. A millionaire does not know such enjoyment. That also is appreciating pence.

Equally I might say that I want only to be practical with doodles, and ultimately that should be enough for anyone.

I have done ample thinking for the season. I came here to listen to the island — and I have listened — but now I want its solo voice. Every sound it makes is sense.

If I hear a dog barking in the night here, something, I know, is wrong. Somewhere there is a human or animal intruder, and the dog does its job. Otherwise, except on musical evenings, I hear little but the occasional amorous or angry cat, or the mice around my house which I chose — having to have one or the other — in preference. They are so small and inoffensive and have such thoughtful conflicts over escaping from a place of fear and wanting to carry along what booty they have found that I find them far more congenial than the cats.

Beyond these our three sounds in the regular night's chorus are the wind, the cicadas and mules. When the wind blows it is like the surf of distant seas as it breaks far above us on the precipice with irregular splashes on the almond leaves. It does not howl and knock us down as on most Aegean islands, but rather provides the muffled drum-roll as background to our most constant sound, the treble harp note of the cicadas. The mules just honk incongruously, pretending to be arriving or departing boats. Sometimes they succeed in their deception and I think that I have heard a genuine steamer hoot, and then I listen for a moment longer and if the horn is overdoing it I realise that I am listening to a mule. And *vice versa*, knowing how easily they can be taken in themselves — I once managed to talk to one around a corner and receive an answer though I nearly did an injury to my lungs — I am sure that they think each boat a far-strayed friend.

The trumpeting of a mule made out of the night's silence is a proper Aegean noise, but one of the most surprising, considering the docility of these animals. I would call them compliant rather than obstinate, and on Amorgós they have good treatment and good characters. I have only seen one hobbled mule during the course of the whole summer, and often one meets them, loaded or unloaded, alone on the way up to the village or grazing by the path, perfectly in command of their direction and routine. I especially like to see Michali's kind attention to his animals and how he always removes their saddles when they come down from Thollária. Their obvious appreciation, rolling in the sand or reclining under trees, makes equally obvious the annoyance of being forced to wait for hours saddled in the sun. When they are resting their expressions are refined, and when they drink they draw in water elegantly, like a person drinking through a straw. Only in their long-distance conversations do they make an exhibition of themselves; perhaps it is this outlet that makes them in general such well-balanced beasts.

The animals, like all people of Aiyiáli, are kindly treated workers, and it is difficult after living here among them not to feel that this is what animals should be. In the Dorset village where my parents live we are the only family that does not keep a dog, and yet I do not think that we are unkindly disposed. When a stray cat made its house in our woodshed and a chaos of the kindling wood, my father advised 'a policy of mild fierceness' in which, as is fairly obvious, the cat won, and my mother, who apologises to a flower if inadvertently she should uproot it with a weed, has no less a kindly attitude. But we have no job for an animal to do and so we have no pets — 'pet' is not a complimentary word to inflict on animals.

I was grateful to a critic, who on reading an early manuscript of mine vetoed a sentence about a girl coming down a path with a dead pigeon, 'stroking its softly sensuous back'. The sensuous quality of dead or dying feathers are an appealing snare in literature, as I have never known so well as when I put this misplacing of emotion into practice by attempting to rescue a wounded wood pigeon which was cowering with a shot wing in my path along a Dorset river bank. It was an ignorant mistake. In our efforts to save and not be saved we both plunged — and it was January — into the river, and an hour later arrived home very wet and bloody, the bird with terror imposed upon its private ability to carry pain to death, and I with a problem which I suspect contained the more of anguish as the evening advanced in the contemplation of what ought to be done.

Living in the country does not necessarily give one country sense. The influx of retired couples, and families in flight from Bournemouth, spend time and money in the nursery gardens in these parts while the indigents chop down their trees where birds gather and threaten vegetables. Our young poplars once incensed our good-natured neighbours who found their cabbages devoured one day. 'Real country people,' they informed us, 'don't grow trees. Them trees, they hibernate the pigeons,' and I am sure that real country people have no dilettante bogglings about leaving a half-dead pigeon to die quietly or putting it quickly out of its pain. But I continue to plant and tend the trees, so perhaps I should not speak adversely of the pets. One cannot be absolutely and unquestionably right.

The end of that evening, fortunately, must vanish beneath the veto, and I will only say that at one split second far too late at night I thought, 'If I could know what is happening now I could understand the universe.' Why aim so high? Possibly I was right, but as I see clearly now there was no possible means by which I could have known, as I cried out, what was happening.

The hole that the mouse is going into is too small for the piece of bread that he is trying to pull with him.

It is very troublesome to find oneself trying to solve the problems of the world.

Hullo, mouse, your bread ration will continue, for I shall be here over the fourteenth after all. I work slowly, the days are passing, and Henry told Anápyros that he could keep me as a hostage if his money did not come.

Part Three
July 1969

CHAPTER TWELVE

The Wrong Time

I LIKE being here. I just like being here. Today was one of the rare occasions when I did not go down at midday to the sea. I arranged my books and papers, used my kitchen, its utensils, and something of my brain. I went out at six to photograph the church of Ayia Triádha and then found that I was running down the mule track for an evening bath. 'Come swimming, Costa!' He smiled from his field, waving, 'You're late today. Never mind,' he said, 'it's better now that it is cool.'

'You're late today,' laughed Irene in the orchard. 'Is this the time to swim?'

'But my brain,' I said, 'was buzzing, and now I'm well, I want to seize a pen.' It was warm cool and I was dripping, and I wanted to shout out on paper, 'I like being here.'

Neither Costa nor Irene meant that I was late for anything when I ran out of the sea on the evening of 4 July, the day after I came back. I was later than usual, they meant, I had not come down for lunch. Before twenty-four hours on the island had passed we could speak of rare occasions and what is usual, that is why I used the verb 'to like' and not 'to love'.

It is great happiness that this is possible after last year's disintegration when September was passing and I became a hostage of Anápyros. The wrong time made Aiyiáli the wrong place, I should have left and had the wrongness in myself. During that last fortnight I could write nothing, not even about Costa's brothers — three of them and two with families — who had come in full holidaying force into my village life. I did no work from that evening when it seemed essential to write about the animals, and my fear was that a change of mood might cause some lasting damage.

While I was completing those last pages I heard a radio, or thought so, in the normally closed half of the house. It was a Sunday and a family party was going on indoors. I had been alarmed beforehand expecting an invasion, but as it turned out my landlord Yorgo had very little interest in his house. He and his wife moved in with his parents at the bottom of the village, and so did Adoni from Salonica with his almost grown-up daughters, and as only Costa moved out of that house it must have been convivial indeed. Costa came and slept up here with Phaní his youngest brother and their nephew Nikita, Yorgo's son; they arrived late every evening and left early every day. That Sunday was the only time when I felt that this balcony and courtyard were imposed upon, and it was almost worth it — extraordinary but true, it was worth it — for the noise. The songs were unaccompanied, traditional in style but unknown to me. Usually one hears the same songs repeated year after year. 'Thollária, Langátha, Potamós...' so Amorgós lyrics do exist. I would have said that they were live but that the tone was so professional. Amorgots are musical but they do not sound like singers in a concert hall.

'Come and join us, Carolina.' It was Phaní standing at the door, but I had grown isolated on paper with the animals and said that I must do another hour's work. And I am dubious about you, Phaní, I might have added, I suspect that you do not have the honour of your island brother and I do not like your hat. Family and neighbours were passing up and down the stairway, the singing was submerged in welcomes and grew dominant again. 'In Langátha, in Thollária, Potamós....' The tune had changed. Could there really be so many island songs? About five minutes after Phaní made his invitation I left the mouse and went.

Surrounded by relations, Adoni sat importantly before a tape-recorder and a microphone. He is plain and simply fat, and of a pale fatness which had been a shock to me when he introduced himself as Costa's brother on the beach. The short cropping of his greyish hair seems to make his head too small above his bulging cheeks. His nineteen-year-old daughter Pepi stood at his shoulder with a simper, high heels and thick hair that is either blond or bleached, while Costa was grinning shyly in his Sunday suit. Adoni began to sing. Adoni was tape-recording his own songs. He had composed the lyrics and the music, and by his voice he justified his name.

Here I saw the warmest-hearted of the mainland brothers. Like the black sheep of a novel who is discovered by a train of clues to be in fact superior to all the white, so Adoni turned out to have all the most attractive qualities to be owned in one who has abandoned his native island home. He has prospered as a wholesale grocer, a wide-range distributor of local produce, in Macedonia, a necessary step to educate these two girls and his son, and he has no blasé feelings about what he left behind. And Pepi, for all her high-heels and diploma to teach French, is equally convinced that Langátha is the best place in the world; very soon I was agreeing gladly to come and see them in the autumn on my way to Istanbul.

Costa's admiration of Adoni bordered on adoration. 'We are all good, and we are like each other. Only Phaní is of a different character. We are good, but Adoni is the best of all of us. He is a better man,' he added fervently, 'than I.'

Every evening the little *platía* at the bottom of the village was dominated by the lively influx of the Roussos family, when all the neighbours crouched and huddled round the ledges to admire Adoni's voice on tape and join the dance, and the normally inconspicuous *magazí* did thriving business. The tape, I think, was more admired than the voice. Only when the dance began did Costa divert light from all the other brothers despite extreme exhaustion at being so sociable for so many days without neglecting work. The only one proficient as a leader, he became in strength and grace a being who could hardly fail to move those who have seen the finest dances throughout Greece. And then, when he had dealt with inspiration, he turned menial and tired again. Every evening it was Costa's shoulder that bore the heavy pot of drinking-water from the bottom of the village to the top while Phaní and Nikita walked beside. 'Why doesn't one of them take it from you for a change?' I asked one night when I walked home with them. 'Bah!' said Costa, 'I can't hand it over. It's sweeter when I carry it.'

Costa felt that I was distinctly better off with neighbours sleeping in the house, and as they only once appeared in daytime I could enjoy the bedtime visit when we sat together on the balcony without feeling overwhelmed. Nikita, a clean young city man, had been born here, delivered in what I call my dressing-room, but his early years have been efficiently weeded from his life. His father, Yorgo, was the last to leave. He was in the forties when he went to Athens and has also left most thoroughly. Although he is my landlord I did not meet him for a week, he was shadowy or absent at the family gatherings, his only purpose on the island was to shoot. He treated Costa like a hireling, informing me that he was rather stupid, and Costa, humbly, might well have agreed for he seemed to find this elder brother a little awe-inspiring. I retaliated by taking close-up photographs of intimate business with the earth. Most people comb their hair and smile when they see a camera; Costa, who is equally enthusiastic, says, 'Shall I plant these tomatoes?' and goes to work convincingly.

Phaní meanwhile was a little too friendly in the early stages, a little too quick to be familiar. Modelling himself successfully on a *nouveau riche* ideal and speaking grandly of business deals in Athens, he might yet have learnt a thing or two of island manners from the one brother left behind. Costa considered it a neighbour's duty to greet me every evening, if I was up or if I was in bed, calling, 'Carolina!' even if my lamp was out, coming in with shellfish, or sitting outside on the windowsill while I roused myself to discuss the topics of the day. Then after a few minutes he would remove himself to sleep. I would not have held a conversation with his brother from among the sheets.

Often our subject of discussion was Henry's money which should have come by then. The weekly boat for Syra, my port for Mykonos, arrived and left, and I had not gone at the right time. Everyone in Aiyiáli aired different opinions about how money comes, how telegraphically, how by post, how much the postman can distribute, and what would happen if I left. Finally I made an expedition to the *Chora* to consult the master minds, to remove myself one day from the house I was misusing and let the mountain absorb a portion of my restlessness on the return.

When one is out of place oneself in what was once the right place one is in danger of jeopardising what was good in it before. I spent evenings alternately at Vassili's and Anápyros' and hated being seen to turn into the mood of Mykonos. 'Come now, Carolina,' they would say, more sensible than I, 'you've worked hard all the summer, it's only reasonable to relax a little now.' But I was in the wrong place at the wrong time.

Sophia and her mother left for Athens, Irene's lessons gave place to preparations for her own departure, Yorgo left for Santorini, and only Vangeli and Michali helped me with that widespread Greek problem, 'How to pass the time'. Vangeli came one morning hot with oratory, 'We don't know when we will go back to school because Greece is in a turmoil. There may be voting for the colonels but it isn't certain yet. And Papandreou has tried to blow up the Acropolis.'

It is all very well to speak of receiving news late. It is I who do that. Even eleven-year-old Vangeli is in touch with the radio. Am I living, I wondered, in an artificial situation after all? Evening after evening Anápyros sat leaning over the back of his *cafenion* chair cross-examining, discoursing, eyes bright with cynical amusement, passing the time by interest in contemporary affairs.

Everyone but I was concerned in the busyness of autumn, the changing over of the seasons, the rolling out of barrels and treading of the grapes. A pandemonium of highly organised activity greeted me when I came down to the harbour one day of clouds lamentable to no one but myself. Almost every able-bodied man was working in concert to put the roof on a new house and finish in one day. They turned, they mixed, they carried, they were ants up and down a gangplank, and every able-bodied man who was not among them was heaving barrels off a caïque from Santorini, ten thousand kilos of fresh tangy must from which enough retsina would be made to supplement our own when that runs out. Vassili was among the first to come down with mules and carry his portion of the rolling load up to his *magazí* where flies gathered in excitement among the intoxicating fumes.

> *If you have the means, friend, drink,*
> *And drink if you have none,*
> *But if you have and do not give*
> *Don't come here to drink.*

The old placard from his father's days hangs as a text in misspelt characters among the shelves of that small department store, Vassili's *magazí*. But no one was banned from his mellow atmosphere through the long, slow-drinking evenings of those shortening autumn days. I thought, if this becomes a habit will it be expected of me next year? Will I expect it of myself? Being on Amorgós, if so, has become something else.

On 13 September, Eve of the festival of Stavrós, the Holy Cross, villagers on mule and foot trouped from Langátha over rock and mountains and across a crumbling ridge of precipice, about which there are dire stories told of one or two who slipped, making their ninety-minute march to celebrate the day with liturgies and heaps of goat and rice. The vertical extremity of a long island is exactly the kind of place where a Greek shepherd would go and find a Holy Cross miraculously. While the sacred relic has been transported to the monastery a little church where the event took place still cowers on its narrow viewpoint towards the Dodecanese, claiming its pilgrims for an annual picnic on this autumn afternoon.

Formerly violin and bouzouki accompanied the goats out here and the celebration continued through the night. That is allowed no longer, perhaps the potential danger had at some time been fulfilled, but as we perched ourselves around the cooking-pot with our bowls perched on our knees, on one safe ledge in vivid light between the sea and sky and I took what I considered must be outstanding photographs, there seemed something to be said for my delay. But my photographs have been a total failure, apparently I never learnt how to wind in the film, and this year I have to leave a week before the festival.

The dance has become domestic in the village with the precipice repassed, yet no one felt like dancing very much, and the musicians sat with drooping instruments in idle hands. Only Marki the cook, who had relaxed by the evening hour into his normal bearing after a sober midday's work, pulled me unsteadily to my feet and the people of Langátha cried out to be amused. It was his feet that were unsteady, mine were just plain dull; he is also much shorter than I am without staggering — we must have made a curious pair.

A dance without *kéfi*, the mood and inspiration, is not a good dance, and no villager will perform it nor put on acts, but wrong things happen in the wrong place and while I had danced with *kéfi* and no shame on the quayside I rather agreed with our policeman when he advised us, 'Don't go rolling on the ground.' I remember this as the climax of my wrongness, yet it must have coincided with the first boat that I missed, and each lost boat condemned me to another week. When I was left listening to another departing hoot and still in residence myself I told Anápyros, 'I am leaving on the next one if the money comes or not.'

He looked at me, I thought, a little suspiciously, but he could not keep me here except by force. And whatever anybody did or tried to do it was inevitable that the money should arrive at the post office in the *Chora* the day after I took my boat. It was returned to me in Athens and I sent it back again, ten thousand drachmas to Anápyros and two thousand to Costa for the sand, and from that time it was of no material consequence that I had stayed too late, the villagers had had some entertainment, the last week of the month was opportune for Mykonos, and yet it was something not easily ejected from the mind.

One month later, in a little town called variously Gidha or Alexandria outside Salonica, Pepi and her sister slept on their

F

parents' floor having put me comfortably to bed. After all my departure from the circle of Aiyiáli was not to be made with any sense of gloom; it was celebrated with an orgy of its native songs as Adoni indulged himself, his family and me, and we ate almonds from the old mayor's almond tree. Adoni is not as beautiful as his voice but he had endearing eyes, their expression is endearing when they smile because they tell the truth. He smiled a lot that night.

'If you don't stay three days next time, Carolina, we will quarrel.' Thank you, but the capacity of my stomach will quarrel if I do. I accept your house, however, as my hail and farewell frontier post in Greece, and let every arrival and departure be accompanied by the songs of Amorgós.

Because of them this spring the island discarded its remoteness and I had no need to sacrifice myself to the *Myrtidiótissa* or any of her sickening cousins again so early merely to ensure my summer's rent. Rather I arrived with news for Costa, 'Greetings from your brothers in Salonica and Athens, I have seen them all.' Adoni nearly wrecked my constitution for the drive to Athens so well I was received, he sent me to find Phaní who took me to find Yorgo, and Yorgo has spoken to his sister-in-law who says that I can use another room if visitors should come. 'Yorgo says that he will write to you about it.' Costa looked impressed.

We are all far friendlier in retrospect than we had been when together here. Phaní and I had parted on the island with cold politeness, but what would have been the point of that in Athens when a common bond could make an hour's meeting warm? And Yorgo, whom I hardly recognised, acted as if his life's first aspirations were to secure my spare room and send me to the island well informed in local news. So when I arrived and spent my first night in the courtyard I knew — and it was of first importance — that I would be able to draw water, since the well has been repaired.

I found a bucket standing ready, the headstone is replaced, the water sweet, and nothing more was needed before the early morning when I went out to find Costa and he came up with the key. He cleared out the rat poison and I found my broom; by eight o'clock I had ejected the year's cobwebs, and from that hour have almost felt surprised when the people of Aiyiáli pause to welcome me. The last two weeks of last year have little to do with anything, and if I am remembered at the festival of Stavrós I shall not be here when called upon to dance. Perhaps for two weeks' wrongness that will be my lifelong ban.

CHAPTER THIRTEEN

Our People

WITH a good deal of discussion with Yorgo's mother and absolutely none with the parents of my little Michali except in reference to eggs I reopened the junior English class on my third day. 'Yorgo's mother' remains the title of my friend the dressmaker in Langátha, who is now a bakeress as well, but it is the second son eleven-year-old Vangeli who has become the ardent English pupil of that family. Yorgo himself has crossed the Athenian frontier for the first time and is all that is lacking in the usual routine. He is staying with relations, and no doubt his initiation to the city is being a full seventeen-year-old experience for he is expected home on every boat in vain. 'There will be a reckoning,' with a look that is mostly of severity, his mother says.

Michali and Vangeli remember everything they learnt last summer, opening doors and windows on instruction, counting spoons and forks and glasses, telling me that I am a woman with perfect confidence. Each was top of his own form this school year, and full of teacher's pride I look forward to the day in ten or twelve years' time when I walk into American Express or Cook's and find one of them grown-up behind the desk. I think that it will be Michali — Vangeli is veering toward more artistic things — then I will be claimed as his 'own person' and I trust that he will organise my affairs in record time.

Mainland meeting always involves a pleasant sort of pride which fortifies that claim on either side. Costa is more than ever 'my person' and I 'his' since I stayed with one of his brothers in the North and drank ouzo with two others in the South, he is fully appreciative of that. And not only has his family extended into mainland life; wandering in Athens towards Omonia shortly before I left I ran into Irene, who looks not out of place now among traffic in the bustling streets. 'Hullo,' we said, 'when are you leaving? Shall we go together to Amorgós again?' We did not have to be excited or bounce about in wild reunion, that had been done before. In early June and the middle of a heatwave I took her with the two Sophias and another cousin for a Sunday picnic at Skiniá, the beach which I connect with foreign friends. But more and more I am giving up connections of that sort; the people that I like and the places that I like are people and places that I like and I shall not corner them.

How we sweated in that car of mine with three on the back seat, and how we laughed at our most obvious island jokes about meeting over muleback and now fighting out of Athens in a Sunday traffic jam. I was sun-bleached, brown, and they — dark-haired — were white. All of them had spent an anxious week acquiring bathing-suits. Two had borrowed from their friends, Irene had gone out and bought one, for Athens is a place to go to school and Amorgós to swim. For a day I made them defy their categories. Sophia's mother sent us off with a banquet of a hamper and I thought, tearing chicken bones apart, 'What nice girls these are. How well they mingle ease, respect and friendliness.' I wondered too if they infect their schoolmates with their island poise and manners which are obviously too strong a part of them to be infected by anybody else. We stopped at Marathon on the return, and Irene won the battle over who should stand ice cream.

The summer time-table of orchard lessons was quickly put in motion too. Michali, building all day long, turning almost single-handed a bungalow into a two-storey house, paused at work to put in a request for as many English lessons as possible. I promised to increase them, at any rate until Sophia comes next month. 'As to that,' he said with a provocative movement of the hands, 'God will pay,' as if he himself were unable to comply. And yet this is the first year that his family are keeping me fed regularly since

Sophia's mother who is detained in Athens used to be in charge of that. It began happening from the beginning that every day one of his girls brings me a cooked meal which often extends into the evening too. If we did have reckoning I should not be down. Sometimes people tell me that I am too much moved by kindness that is due, but it would be a poor thing if one were only grateful for what one is given in excess. Now my gratitude goes chiefly to the way in which Michali palms off on to God what he is doing perfectly well himself. I made one speech to him three years ago, and am sure that it will not be heard again. That is not the point — it is not even relevant any more.

Breaking off in a lesson at the end of last year's summer, Irene said, 'I always think of this as your house now.'

'Could you have rented it?' I asked. 'Did other people ask for it?'

'We could have but we didn't want to.' I had been right in my prediction that I would not be moved around. Of course it was a matter of honour once there were two sisters to take English lessons, but it was this that was notable and generous, none of the family had told me, 'We could have earned this money or that money,' none had bragged about it. They knew that I would know, and only under provocation was it lightly said.

Irene's remark was precipitated simply by two hats, catching her attention on the wall where I had hung them on two nails in the orchard cottage, broad-brimmed and twinlike side by side. Henry's and Catherine's, they had spent the winter there in polythene, and though their owners have probably forgotten them they are likely to wait another year to be reclaimed. I do not normally care much for objects, I mean for the having, for the ownership. I like buying and using what is functional and beautiful at once, but those dumps deposited about the place are so consistently dispersed by some mysterious, evaporating winds that I prefer to own the minimum. I do not even worry much about the losing, for really there are no possessions in this world, rather everything is hired for a time, and my chief anger over the loss of my Vienoula rug which would have matched the mayor's blue rafters is directed at myself for being angry; I will find a way to master that. But the hats threatened to ruin my siesta by suddenly asserting their personal significance. They were left casually behind and casually found again, and so were the remains of a bottle of shampoo, a bag of detergent and a very old dress which I told Irene had better be a rag — they have attached us to the place. This is a meaning of being a part of all that one has met.

Perhaps it is because Greek is my first working language here that I incline towards the possessive adjective while repudiating possessions simultaneously. 'My village', 'my house', 'my Irene' and 'my boys' as a translation from the Greek are places and people with whom one has connection, they are one's own by association rather than by actual ownership, a pleasing way of having things. 'My Vangeli' is a child whom I teach, a person in my life, I may address him so, 'Vangeli *mou*', just as Sophia's mother sometimes calls me, 'Carolina *mou*'. It is unobjectionably the English 'dear' used of someone for whom one is responsible. And whatever happens — though holes fall out of life and circumstances change — relationship remains a relationship, and in both cases Henry and Catherine are included on my side.

So the shampoo remained, and the hats remained, and the hats are what I like because they are not mine but part of my extension in Aiyiáli. 'Where is Jason?' everybody asks me. 'When is your brother coming?'

'Unfortunately next summer, they can't manage it this year. They've just adopted a new baby, two months old and premature. What are we to do with "Julian" in Greek?' No one can answer that. 'And my father was very ill last winter so Henry is going home to visit him.' All this is very proper and commendable. They will come next year and that will be the same. This summer, next summer, while you are having it what is the difference? The hats are waiting on the wall, and a pile of sand is waiting on the mountainside where Henry's forehead had painfully demanded shelter from the sun.

When I climbed up on my return to the plot inside his corner posts I thought for one faithless moment, 'Are the thousand bucketfuls of sand a myth?' I could not have believed it except that I was there and no sand was. The deception lay in camouflage. Costa has deposited his thousand buckets and thrown on top a small fieldful of gorse, and stones on that. The sand has been rained through and not escaped, it is a new mound in the humpy mountainside, and the only thing that worries me is that it sprawls out all over the one area which is flat enough to put a house.

The problem is becoming imminent for Henry writes that he may send me plans for something to be started, and I am to find out all I can about materials and techniques. So after all we are digging in our feet. Meanwhile one-legged Anápyros died at Easter, he will discourse on politics no more. It was said that he loved his money too much to attend to doctors — I hope that we were in no way responsible. I must admit that my first thought was whether our mock contract is mocker than before, but Henry does not seem over-anxious about that. 'If a thousand buckets of sand squatting on the site does not establish my right I do not know what would.' I rather felt that if his rights were questioned I could produce two hats.

In spite of general loving kindness, for the first time on this island I have been severely reprimanded. I was going to fetch wine from the harbour at noon my second day and, knowing the difference between the beach and a few houses a hundred yards from the beach when you are in Aiyiáli, I robed myself in a towel dress before setting foot among them. Kyria Maria ejected me from her *magazí* with piercing fury. I must admit that my towel dress is not much longer than a shirt.

'What will you do?' I shouted, since shouting was the order, 'when you get tourists here? What do you do in any case when people pass from the hotel?' Not all of them are scrupulous about what is left exposed. But Kyria Maria is more interested in morals than in tourists, more concerned with the ideas that may infect both men and girls, and her shrieks were disturbingly voluble as I retreated down the quay. She is the only one who would object down here, or objecting say so, and liking her as I do and remembering how I shared her supper the night before I left last year, I am loath to have a quarrel there. In the evening I apologised 'for doing something which you didn't like', which was as far as I would go, and was generally informed that she was only speaking as a mother would. God and our mothers, on what more influential people can we rest our arguments? I could not bring myself to tell her how my own mother would be far too diffident to make more than the gentlest hint of criticism about her children's clothes.

I think I shall take it as a compliment that she does not treat me with the tight-mouthed forebearance that she would give to the hotel residents. If the give and take of 'my people' is to be used between me and the islanders I must have their barks as well. The next day Kyria Maria was in an exceptionally good humour — almost merry — perhaps I should insult her once a month. She made me judge her ouzo, one brand from Athens and one from Mytilene which I preferred because it has more kick, bringing with it her small olives, 'the fruits of Amorgós', thus managing to put some note of pride into the island's present lack of almost anything that can be picked off trees.

I wondered, since bills are always interesting in Greece for their reflection on the frame of mind, how much my bill would be. This year each *magazí* throughout Aiyiáli has impressed itself with a catalogue of prices on the wall, each giving the same items regardless of what is available, and the same prices whether or not they are the same. This neat little plaque which does no harm to anyone is a new effect of military government. Ouzo, which used to be one drachma or one fifty has graduated to one eighty on the wall, or two drachmas with *mezé*, the olive or whatever titbits there may be that go along with it. In practice I find that ouzo is one fifty or two depending on the shop, while the *mezé*, as before, depends on mood. When Kyria Maria pronounced three drachmas for two day's drinks each time with olives, she had also pronounced her full forgiveness.

After the incident of the towel dress, and thinking what our beach has and does not have, I decided that it is indispensible for Michali to open a little *magazí* where customers can drink and eat something very simple under bamboos or under trees in bathing-wear or not. I told Irene and the project immediately absorbed a grammar lesson. 'I like conversation,' she exclaimed, and I was longing to hover over the driving-in of the first post.

It is the dedication to learning, and perhaps such things as being her father's workman, that preserves the child in Irene at fifteen and one month, but this has nothing to do with her efficiency, and a great deal of that is to be demanded of her soon. Her mother is leaving for Syra and Athens with the baby Kianoula, whose name is a practical and pretty way of dealing with 'Efdhokía Ioanna', to take her to the doctor for treatment for her bandy legs. Apart from the language it must be for her like travelling to a foreign land, a hard sacrifice of time and money in these busy summer days. Often in villages and on islands deformities are accepted, like dark hair or fair hair, as things that people have. I am glad that this family think it important for the baby to be sent to Athens on account of bandy legs.

At first I wronged Michali by thinking that they were sending Kianoula to Syra for the doctor there. The stop at Syra is to collect insurance papers, and then the mother will take her on to Athens for treatment which may last about a month. Only the best, and rightly, is good enough in serious matters of doctoring for his girls, and Michali is too well organised to leave it to God to pay for things like that.

Among these people uncalculated giving can only be a pleasure. In schools I was a mediocre teacher with pay-day as the strongest motive, but here I find these vital and enthusiastic children worth more than any reckoning can reach. Irene having jumped another year, completing six in three, remains one of the top students in her class and has informed me — for she makes such decisions — that twice a week this summer we are to read *Jane Eyre*. And I cannot claim a great amount of laurels for her success, though I have helped, when I think how her sister was achieving the same sort of disregarding of years' classes before I taught her anything.

Poor girl, she was the only one to suffer from my irritation when she first came into my hands, and I cannot tell why, but now we have the ease together that I have been having with Irene since the day she learnt the alphabet. At Skiniá we played ball together in the sea.

CHAPTER FOURTEEN

Barnacles

THIS year our letters are delivered more spasmodically than before, since one of the two former postmen has given up with heart failure and is not to be replaced. I was sorry to hear the news but not surprised. The postal system has always been beyond me. Continually new aspects expose themselves which I did not know about. All last year, and the first year that I came, I received my letters from Miki's *cafenion* at the harbour thinking that I got them earlier that way since the postman passes in the early afternoon. It was not until the last week of the second season that a revelation fell, my instructions had been interpreted as, 'Carolina wants her letters at the harbour if the postman misses her on his Aiyiáli round.' Kind, spectacled Vangeli had taken up my letters to Langátha in case he saw me there, and once I did pass him on the way down for an evening swim after a day at home and he handed me a postcard from his mule. For the sake of that the rest of my whole summer's correspondence toured the mountain to Thollária, spent the night there and was brought down again to Miki's the next day. It hardly seemed to make a difference when letters take up to a fortnight to arrive in any case.

Miki meanwhile had solved another of the communication problems by himself. On the publication of my first book I was to receive a greetings telegram and my editor had thoughtfully written long before to let me know what it would be and when it would be sent. I told Miki that I was expecting it, I knew the contents, and there was no reason why he should send for me. Apparently, because of previous experience I was over-emphatic in my speech; he decided that this would be good future policy and took to housing any telegrams until I happened to pass by. I could rouse myself, I suppose, and say that this year I want delivery, but there again, when letters are so rare and unconcerned with postmarks the possibility of a telegram on any day at passing-by time is something like excess.

By fortunate accident one afternoon I emerged from my siesta early. I just happened to be on the beach when a family party passed by and informed me that the remaining postman had brought me a remittance and I should be down on the quay to collect it the next day at eight o'clock. Hoping to keep my travellers' cheques for future journeys I had already begun swapping a few English pound notes with the president for drachmas, to be swapped back again. It was a great relief. Probably if I had not been on the beach then I would have missed the money for the best part of a week.

However, there it was circling the mountains and I did not want to be down early in the morning, so I took to the steep path for Thollária from the far end of the beach to make the postman's round in the opposite direction, one infallible method of meeting him somewhere. Five minutes after arriving I heard the postman's horn, and went up to meet him in the *magazí* which is his village base. A ludicrous thought occurred to me, 'He's a new man in Aiyiáli, he doesn't know me, suppose before handing me three thousand drachmas he asks to see my passport....' But I was right in seeing this as ludicrous. Then as I set out for Langátha before darkness fell I was struck by another equally outlandish thought, 'There are places in the world where one would never put forty pounds publicly into one's purse and disappear in twilight along a lonely mountain path.'

The paradox of our communications becomes either infuriating or hilarious — and I usually feel the latter — on clear days. Out there on the horizon is Mykonos, I could see it if Naxos were not in the way, and during my fortnight on Platí Yialó in June, I used to make out the not-so-distant lines of Amorgós. And all my good friends there, those who, if they can make the immense effort, will materialise, are virtually as far from me as if they were living on the Ionian Isles. Only if I shout loud enough I might be heard — sometimes I feel that. 'I have an extra room for you. Do you hear that? Come! They all promise to do so later in the month, such things are possible and part of this year's scheme. 'Don't send letters! Come!'

Out there where I am looking — glad not to be there at this season but enjoying looking — a little shrine on the road to Anomerá in the middle of the island marks the spot of Mykonos' third fatal accident. Drunken driving is not known there as different from any other kind of driving, rather the new fleet of motor cycles is still taken as a speedy form of donkey with the added joy of being noisier. Athanássios Kousathanás O Petinós, 'The Cock', proprietor of the taverna which is my home base on Platí Yialó, was the victim when three rode home together on one motor cycle from a winter festival, and another rock on our landscape disappeared. The shrine contains his photograph and his epitaph is formidable on a sign beside it, 'Drivers! Don't go fast! Don't get drunk!'

Stavroula his widow, now in black for eighteen months, is still hard-worked at the taverna which grew past his comprehension into a hotel and has three sons to run it, all of whom know better than he ever did about the incongruous modern ways which killed him in the end. In spite of drudgery and mourning she had an occasion of great happiness in June; her first grandson, five-day-old Athanássios, named after the old man, was brought down to the beach. The next week Marina from the taverna at the far end received her own first grandson, and each baby has a two-year-old blonde sister, Marina and Stavroula respectively, and no one could work out a system of families and generations more methodically, more pleasing in its precise geometry than that which has — I can only say divinely — come about.

Living in a cottage in the orchard for a fortnight of my favourite month, eating supper with the family who were not too busy yet to sit down together once a day, I was seized with the joy of the rightness of their simple relationships, I could not be cynical about the rows of beach umbrellas, the pullman buses, and the new acquisition of a telephone.

'So you're leaving us for Amorgós?' they say.

'Yes, you know that it would drive me crazy here next month.' They are not insulted, they know what I mean. Loving and liking have become my theme this summer, they are better feelings than dislike and hate, they are easy to achieve if one can only be, at the right time, in the right place. My own mistakes and some two-way abuse once made life down there impossible, but I have learnt that timing, tolerance and balance can obliterate all that formerly was wrong.

Stavroula, exhausted from the day's work, subsided from the table and lay down in the gravel with her head propped up among the flowers growing around the pillar in the middle of our outdoor floor. One day I will make a point when writing not to tread on the same ground, but the same ground that evening was so funny, and it really was the ground. Our habitual drinker, the lean farmer Vassili, tottered up and slid on to the gravel with his head in black Stavroula's lap. 'What's this!' The widow was jerked forcibly awake, and chortling in her month's good humour did not throw him off. Theodorí, the eldest son, arrived dead sober from the village and threw himself down too, turning the dusty pair into a line of figures in the dust.

Grovelling in the gravel! Yanni, the young father, found that the most relaxing place to hug and play with his little Stavroula an hour earlier. Love in the gravel! Theodorí is embracing the confused Vassili now. The drunkard's aged father, watchdog on such wanderings, sits squarking his severities from the rear, and Stavroula bids me, 'Give Vassili a glass of wine.' The retsina is always mine these days. Since the taverna has reverted to the bottled kind I bring down a flagon from the village and am glad to do so, for even Stavroula, who is a serious person, is willing to be treated to one small glass at night, a rare indulgence in her hard-working life. So I give Vassili a glass and she, heaving her head from the flowers protestingly, lets forth a torrent of abuse. 'He's drunk, and you are giving him more wine! How are we going to get him home?' I am bewildered as her shrieks fly through the air. 'That's for his father,' she whispers with a wink, 'give him another, he's my cousin. Carolina!' she yells as I comply, 'Stop that! Stop giving Vassili wine!' And the exhausted widow and the drunken farmer and the giant Theodorí lie grovelling and loving in the gravel, and meanwhile, so I discovered, the ricketty old father has had a quick double cognac in the shop.

There is no wind tonight to blow away the images that come straight from Mykonos. This is our first day of real *boundtsa*, the dead calm which turns the sea to oil, breeds drowsiness of body and, in some dissociated way, alertness of the mind. Say what I may about possessions the new acquisition of a little outdoor furniture from Athens transforms *boundtsa* days, but if they are lost tomorrow they have been worth the bringing for this one occasion as a time to be retained. I have remembered barnacles and a rock from a quayside conversation as a simile for love. A large rock has room for many barnacles, and each barnacle is attached in its own right. No love is less for another love one has, capacities grow greater, they cherish and they add. Loving is not infatuation, loving is not romantic, loving is not necessarily 'being in love with' any one or any thing. 'To love', I think, should be used warily for places, I do not 'love Greece', I am not 'in love with Greece', but Greece is a place where I understand what is valuable in love. Writing now by lamplight in the *boundtsa* night when the flame is undisturbed, and looking out into that night towards the world, I acknowledge barnacles. My love is not made less by quantity, each love that I have retains its power and value, and my aim is not to spend my life loving the people whom I love, for that will happen anyway, but to expand, to allow my love to grow.

When a friend of mine in Athens told me that she despised ninety-eight per cent of humanity I suddenly remembered my later schooldays and much more recent years when it was easy to take pride in a melancholy nature and an overdose of scorn. I told her, 'That means you have a superiority complex, or else you hate yourself.' I had just decided that people are wonderful, I was enchanted, it was the achievement of my life. Again, one of the English teachers in Chalkís, an American girl having her first view of Greece from a provincial town, asked me how I could tolerate living in this country basically alone. She, provocative in looks and figure, has suffered from a despicable reaction everywhere she goes, and I know what she means, it is outrageous that some impudent young man or boy should have the power to humiliate one. But I said that I had learnt to manage somehow to avoid the times and places where I provoke what I dislike, the problem is not more difficult than that.

I also think that since it is clearly unusual to abominate squealing crowds and litter over beaches, transistors over ancient ruins, wolf calls on street corners and juke boxes on wild waterfronts, it is probably presumptuous to suppose that the ten per cent are 'right' in preferring opposites. Let the world go on, and I will not go to the beach from Athens on a Sunday, let the world go on and I will not go to Platí Yialó in August. Rather than that I come to the mayor's house, but why should I suppose that my own discrimination is superior to the rest?

I should hate it to be said that what I say of loving indicates that I see the world through rose-coloured spectacles or anything so corny. If I have a warm feeling every evening when I come panting up the back street past Vassili's shop and see the good and easy faces relaxing up the steps, and if I pause to drink a glass of wine among them, or just pause, they have their work and I have mine, we do not pass the time of day together, I rarely sit for more than half an hour, rarely for so long. Knowing that they are there I am saved from calling myself a hermit on this island, but we are far more easy in our meetings than effusive. Greece has made me every year less romantic than the first year that I came. I am perfectly aware of the capacity of half the people that I write about for, say, getting the better of foreigners, or any deficiencies you please. I am inclined, especially when guiding friends, to be ferocious over bills and service at tavernas or whatever I see reasonable in their complaints, but what is to be liked is for liking, and I do not think that deficiencies in a person have much to do with his good qualities.

At the end of June I left my car in Panagítsa, the Euboian village where I lived when teaching in Chalkís. The intermingling leaves of a vine and mulberry tree by the taverna make the shade to solve a summer parking problem and preserve the link with a place where I have learnt that pure, unreasoning affection has no need of common ground. Circumstances make certain people 'one's own people' and then affection grows — preferences about their characters and habits are too hampering for love. Here I spent three final days of driving teachers out to beaches, driving village children for an evening's outing, driving friends home after dinner, until, like Cinderella on the stroke of midnight, I drew up beneath my vine and then it was July and my insurance had expired; we had had happy days.

I was staying in one of the rooms attached to the house where I had lived before, and was roused repeatedly from semi-sleep by the urgency which had been attacking me again of writing late-night messages. On my last night in Panagítsa I had to turn on the light and find a pen that it should be recorded, 'I love to love and I love being loved. I like to like and I like being liked.' It did seem a little comic in the morning, but I decided that it had more sense than other notes. I could not call it shame nor an admission to say that there is great happiness involved when liking and loving are reciprocal, and happiness does good to everyone.

CHAPTER FIFTEEN

The Chora

On the morning of the twelfth I was handed a letter in Langátha — a rare event but I have given up asking questions — and ten minutes later was celebrating the home news with Vassili; Catherine is going to have a baby in February. I was celebrating largely with laughter, and Vassili joined in too to hear my mother's words. 'Henry,' who has been with her in Dorset, 'was a little dazed because they had only just got No. 2 rather suddenly and unexpectedly, and the news that No. 3 is already on the way is a bit startling. It means that for a brief space they will have three under two.' Henry and Catherine do things not at all or thoroughly, at present they are having babies, they are prolific, I could make luscious similes about ripe fruit — perhaps I won't. Vassili thought the idea delightful, so did Stephanáki, but does this mean that they will not be able to come here next year? Why not? We shall have three backs for the hill.

I walked on laughing, wanting to see those backs in use immediately, and there was Costa riding up. He jumped off urgently and his two mules ambled on alone. Had I been discussing building as instructed? When would I write to Henry? Had I seen Adoni Gavalá? He — in Costa's opinion — was less expensive than the other builders and as good. 'He's working now on a house behind Michali's orchard, go and see him. Hurry, he may leave.'

'I will go,' I said, 'and do you know, Catherine is going to have a baby in the winter, she is — what's the word?' I groped for it.

'Pregnant, you mean?' he cried, indicating a round stomach on his own lean front. '*Kaló ríziko!* — good rooting! — But hurry

Carolina, Adoni will leave soon, he can show you the foundations he is working on, to see how you like them.' Babies and foundations, somehow the day's combination was appropriate. *Kaló ríziko!* That is the greeting for them both.

Adoni had left by the time I found his place of work, but I could not see that this mattered very much since he is a Langátha man and the sight of some foundations to my unknowledgeable eyes would not have added greatly to the evening's conversation which was easily contrived. In obedience to Costa I gathered a mass of information to report to the family in Washington State who are at the moment more interested in babies I am sure. But never mind, they have a large capacity. Henry should be encouraged to hear the builder's comment about the early placing of the sand, 'And I said to myself, "That must be one who knows".'

Costa called in afterwards to inquire about this discussion, verifying that the substance had tallied with what he himself had said. 'That's what I told you, your brother can have stone if he wants it, but it will cost him twice as much, or three times, it would have to be brought over from the other side. Write and tell him that,' and then he said it all again. Costa is always under the impression that no one can understand instructions — his father is going deaf I think — unless they are repeated for as long as the ouzo or the coffee lasts and five minutes afterwards. He repeats with the vigour of a politician canvassing, of the rhetorician who convinces that life depends upon his cause, and each sentence is as full of feeling as the first.

One reason for his urgency at that particular moment was that he knew my intention of closing enquiries with a visit to the *Chora* and Katápola. There after all sit the powers of the island, there two summer houses have been built for foreigners, in all likelihood I should discover some vital piece of information which in Aiyiáli would never come into our heads. At any rate it made a good reason for a long-distance quest for lemons, for the annual greetings in the capital and a visit to my English friends, the Barretts, who ought never to have been left out of my island writing for so long. My tone would be unpardonably possessive if I did not immediately admit that there is a young English couple on Amorgós who are far more part of it than I. If any foreigners are entitled to the term of residents they are, for as a family with two small children they have stayed through winters here.

When I first came to Amorgós on the crazy boat from Syra which drew only half a dozen foreigners and a few more Greeks, the one couple who did not disembark at any of the more likely places were bound to attract my attention, and vice versa, I did not get off and I attracted theirs. I was going to the island with an inkling that this would be the answer to a private problem; they, on exactly the same day and also after years in Greece, were solving a problem of their own. It was impossible, having landed, that we should not keep meeting during the three days that I spent based at Katápola, we appreciated what looked like kindred spirit but with a deep suspicion. 'It's clear that we like the same things,' we smiled with a reservation which contained the right to resent what we were saying when we ran into each other at the monastery.

The second time that I came to Amorgós, on my next year's prospective tour, I met the Barretts on the boat again. It seemed that there was some outside force at work which concentrated on throwing us together, but we were thrown now with a mountain range between us, our toes were far too far apart for treading on and we could immediately settle down to being friends.

Susan Barrett has a novel, *Jam Today*, in proof, and a second under contract before this first is out. Peter had his third exhibition of painting in London in the winter, and for one convivial evening Amorgós was vital in the area of Marble Arch while a large proportion of the English people who have visited the island — so we told each other — drank and reminisced together with esoteric consciousness. The house which they have taken outside Katápola is more of a creative seat than my old mayor's.

The last time that I saw them here turned into one of those experiences which mercifully become a lasting pleasure for their retrospective agony. Peter and Susie arrived sweating in Langátha at the end of a hot windless morning last September just before I left, returning a visit which I had made the month before. They had chosen a day to coincide with a caïque for their return, and in the evening we went down to the quay to wait for it over supper at the muleteers' *magazí* where what began as a leisurely hour became anxiously long. It was late, but it did come. The trouble was that Captain Dimitri had decided to make Santorini his next stop. Peter and Susie, already slightly blistered but anxious for their children, took to the mountain with no moon at ten o'clock. I was aghast, I felt as I saw them bravely disappearing that in some way the disaster was my fault — I was sure they would be lost. But a thunder-storm came up and it seemed likely that, if nothing else, the lightning would indicate their path.

If claustrophobia is the disease of islands we do not suffer from it here, where even compatriots are divided by such long-distance obstacles. On the mountain beyond Potamós we cross a frontier.

To pedestrians from Aiyiáli our little *Chora* is revealed as a great metropolis with its electricity, its eggs in almost every shop, its genuine post office and a few foreigners. I made my expedition, and like Irene I did not go in a car but I did see one. I walked down into Katápola rather than wait three hours for transport, but admiring the fact that if I wanted to I could. I bought some plums, I bought some eggs, I bought two tins of stuffed vine leaves and three of sardines with hot peppers in 'piquant sauce'. I got very excited but I could not find a lemon, Katápola is as deprived of lemons as we are. And it had rained the day before while we just had some clouds, four times and hard.

The day was extraordinary for conversation, I spoke English, I met more English people at the Barretts' than I could sort out, I drank Nescafé, I saw a girl in bright red lipstick — a strange sight in an island situation at this time of year. Summer makes one's complexion simply summerlike, it is only the winter that needs to give the matter thought. Their ultimate aim, so Peter told me as we sat on the quayside among a dozen foreigners all waiting or watching for the boat, is to come here in the winter and leave the slightly trodden shore for England in July. I felt almost a superficial foreigner. They should see Mykonos. But I did well to put myself in new surroundings for a day; it shook me into remembering such things as permits if a house is to be built. Concrete foundations and brick walls are the unanimous decision, but you can't just go and do it when you come to think of it. An expedition to Syra or Naxos might be required for the paperwork.

I would not have gone back over those mountains on the same day for money, so I was truly impressed in my satisfied exhaustion by the Barretts' parental love. One way is enough. But they themselves look back on that night of uncalculated walking with happy haziness. Susie swears that she can remember nothing until they stumbled downhill from the *Chora* with lightning in their path. And now there is less than this mountain range between us for they have acquired a small caïque and can come to Aiyiáli under their own steam in an hour and a half. This has encouraged our decision that they should come and stay with me over the formidable fifteenth of August, the Virgin's festival — any proper inhabitant receives friends or relations at that time. I am hardly sure whether I am doing mine a kindness or insuring moral support and properness, but they are likely to consider the day itself a reasonable tax on the pleasure of shredding garlic on the Eve.

After hours on the mountain, the *Philipos* for so short a journey was a pleasure trip. There on board was our own *tachidhrómos* who has, I trust, pillows from Athens and my first developed film. There I succeeded in wangling one lemon from the kitchen. And there — suddenly I was caught up in handshake and embrace — was Sophia and her mother and a fascination of items of their two months' baggage, July in Athens had forced them to change plans. Suitcases, bags, baskets, sacks were gathered in mounds as we approached Aiyiáli's lights. Four round loaves of city bread, to which I was bound to be subjected for the next few days, were crammed on top of other provisions in a lumpy sack and barely — just — tied up. I grasped a plate-rack in my empty hand as the caïque came out, and somehow or other everything was accommodated on the seething deck. The time of Athenian relatives has begun.

The *platía* had not closed down when I trudged into Langátha with my rather sore feet, my stuffed vine leaves and sardines. Vangelió brought me wine and water quickly while the scribe looked on and, hearing that I had gone to Katápola by foot, clicked with his tongue, 'Tch, Tch.' But if he disapproves so greatly of people going, and voluntarily, for long mountain walks, I hope he paid no attention to my answers to Vangelió's cross-examination about the outside news, the tourists and the weather and the shops. I think that Langátha would hardly be a proper village without one member to frown on foreigners.

I bought plums, I told them, in the *Chora*, but before one day had passed for the first time this summer I found plums on our own quay in large supply. And the president's shop had a bowl full of fresh eggs. Aiyiáli has asserted itself, it is good enough for me, I have not yet opened one tin here of anything but marmalade. The journey was fun, that was its reason — reason enough for anything — here we even dispense with the necessity of going off to Naxos for a building permit, or any such of Katápola's exorbitant ideas.

'I can give you a permit here myself,' our policeman said when I called by, 'if your ceilings are to be made of wood or of bamboo.' This must be one definition of a private dwelling; it is also one of the best things I have heard since I arrived. He did not ask about the number of square metres, or metres from the sea, he asked me if we are going to make our ceiling of bamboo or wood. Of course we are.

Having dealt with these official matters, the policeman asked about my work, and on hearing that what he started off has become a book based on the village informed me that he can help again. He knows a lot of facts, dates and statistics, for though he does not know about a writer's work he was always good at essays so he remembers what he learns. We agreed to have a meeting 'sometime' soon, and I have no doubt that he will be able to produce, in white or gold, some more goat's teeth.

Plans in triplicate are needed next, and even if the baby-minded family respond at once the month will pass. Having dealt with information I settled back into the routine of Aiyiáli's timelessness. Sophia's mother is my cook, Yorgo has arrived at last, Costaki the priest's grandson has been added, strictly for short hours, to my village lessons, and I will not accept another pupil however many virgins his weeping, widowed grandmother may invoke.

I was glad, however, that I had given in about Costaki when I discovered that he is the grandson of the priest. That benign and bearded figure is so appropriate an onlooker from his hub-of-the-village balcony, it has been my ambition since I came here to sit up there with him. Now, thanks to Costaki that has been achieved. He is a little deaf and has not much conversation, and I decided that the best way to take our village priest is to admire his face in its superior position from below and to receive the patriarchal greeting or the blessing whenever it is cheerfully bestowed. But now, 'How is Costaki's English?' that too can be added, and he will probably join the troupes next month who send their children with too many figs.

CHAPTER SIXTEEN

Snowballs

SOMETIMES it amuses me on the mule track on the way up to Langátha to think of some other scene elsewhere, as far removed from mules as possible, and to discover by a process of following the links along a chain that it originated from these stones among the donkey dung and doodles that I am walking on. My great moment of pride this year, for instance, occurred during the first week of May when I had just arrived from England and the Ambassador's chauffeur, unprovoked, offered to buy my car. It was parked inside the precincts of the British Embassy looking so elegant that I was as ecstatic as a Greek mother seeing her child in his new Sunday suit. I had had its dents undented, and though not even the chauffeur's chauffeur — if there were one — could have felt covetous by any means the day before since the mutilation of midges and the like is horrible on the way, it had now been so professionally cleaned that I had no shame in parking it beside the Ambassador's. What may seem out of keeping, but is not so at all, is that it is this village, this mule track, which is responsible.

Being in the right place at the right time gears one's movements toward other right places at their own right times. Langátha was quick to expand on possibilities, it was in the first three weeks of my first summer here that I went dutifully to the Panayía, the Virgin Mary's church, on her day of festival, was surprised to see another foreigner relaxing in the shade, and soon had a friend in Freya Stark. Obscure places are most effortless and interesting for meetings; it would be eccentric behaviour, if not offensive, for two foreigners to meet on village territory and not to talk.

One short conversation, a subsequent lunch and afternoon together before she left her hotel on the quay, and the beginnings of a spasmodic correspondence prompted a letter over a year later in which Freya invited me to come and help put her papers and photographs in order for a month. I replied by cable from Dorset that I would set out immediately, and having once been trained to work for her gained a recurrent job. Her Italian house is well placed for my journeys, half-way along my road to England; it was there last November that I met Sir Michael Stewart, the British Ambassador in Athens, and the train of events explains itself. When I crossed the frontier this spring I stayed first with Costa's brother Adoni outside Salonica and then, on coming into Athens, with the Stewarts. Amorgós received me well in Greece.

Sir Michael had already organised the beginning of my working year, sending me off to Spetsai beyond Hydra in the Saronic Gulf. Here I had a ten-day job which financially speaking had its summer influence, and is also a pleasure to be repeated when I leave Amorgós. My American employer on his retirement came to the island with his wife to build a house which they have made their permanent residence. Externally, from land and sea, it can be mistaken for some old captain's house among the village architecture, but inside the furnishings are clearly too comfortable for that, the books too many, the bathrooms far remote, and yet there is a harmony between each article and the walls. As shipowners, artists, diplomats and secretaries come in no one does not feel that he is the most welcome visitor received, no one is not moved by the beauty that he sees. In these surroundings I did a little 'typing editing', played scrabble, went on boat trips with an ice-jar in the picnic hamper, drank generous amounts of highly un-Greek spirits, and was aware the whole time in the amused and appreciative background of my mind how strangely links are put together and chains made. Offered a lift to Athens by private aeroplane I was smiling privately to think, 'The mule track from Langátha is responsible.'

Everything that passes through my life is something in my

life. The people are, Langátha is, and all of them are part of one another.

What is outgoing must also be incoming; there would be no point in what I am saying if it were merely an extension of my private life. My hostess made it an aim to come to Amorgós this summer, and I think that if she turned up here tonight she would not make complaint about the amenities of the mayor's house, only mongrels would do that. This then became my own aim for the season, to put back into the island what I have taken out of it, to let it gain from what it gave. If any one person whom I met on Spetsai should come and see Aiyiáli, investing in a plot of land or ordering a meal, that aim would be fulfilled. I meet A on an island who introduces me to B who introduces me to C who comes back to the island and helps it on its way; it is a chapter in the history of the world, it is an ending to my story, and if it does not happen now, if it is D or E who comes next year my story is some pages longer, that is all. If my achievement of the year is my friends' considering timetables and feeling thwarted it is still something; I have pushed the snowball which may eventually roll over my own back.

The Spetsai household had a notably good cook, and maids who like Freya Stark's Bertilla did everything they did with deferential friendliness — or friendly deference. Freya is appalled that their counterpart in England has almost disappeared, not only because as an intellectual person she finds domestic chores a waste of time, but because 'service is one of the best of human relationships,' and we have lost our capacity to deal with it. Having had servants all her life, regardless of some years of poverty, she has the authority to state that no sense of superiority or inferiority is attached, but rather one of mutual responsibility, a give and take. The employer and employed are different people, helping each other by their different forms of work, one gives orders but the one who obeys is not 'inferior'. Certainly from the moment of entering her house one would feel it unnatural not to be waited on, but when I tell Freya that as English houses are constructed nowadays we would not know where to put a servant

Snowballs

if we had one I have merely hit the heart of her complaint. In adjusting ourselves to a life without servants during and after the last war we did well, for we were forced into the change: in saying now that we are better off without them, in replacing them with gadgets, we are shirking a responsibility, we are caging ourselves in little citadels, isolating ourselves from the possibility of playing our part in this relationship. When I am in her house I often find myself agreeing, and then I think, 'Must I be selfish if I do not want a maid?' I doubt if I shall ever have one, but I am determined neither to lose nor cause a loss, and if each little citadel-owner outgoes in some direction he may perhaps replace what is thrown out.

Service is such a basic question in the history of the world that I am more than ever grateful to the Virgin of Langátha for this enlargement, with discussion, of first-hand experience. One evening in Vassili's *magazí* I recounted to his wife the whole train of these events, and we gloated over our pleasure in agreeing how far the village can stretch its influence. Her name is Eleftheria, Freedom, and I talk freely in her company. Rather than the remoteness of the subject, work prevented me from continuing the story, but I might have told her how the island can also have effect upon more abstract things. She would have understood my meaning about Athenian attitude.

When I moved from the Embassy and Spetsai to my hotel in Makrianni I discovered that Julia's taverna has turned from Moon to Star, *To Phengári* to *T'Astéri* and moved a mile down the road. One ought always to be prepared for these events, one ought to anticipate the holes which fall out where the ground was firm, I am training myself towards the day when my landlord takes up residence in the mayor's house, I remind myself continually that I am probably cutting my own throat by putting Langátha on the map, I try to train myself to expect nothing but it is difficult. It is very difficult at the moment when the void yawns up to grasp from past experience that somehow or other voids get filled. Julia and Vassili are still being Julia and Vassili, and not so far away, but the home dining-room has gone. Every evening spent there is an expedition, a new reunion, to be driven to, and driven away from with rigid concentration at the wheel. I became increasingly attached to a straightforward taverna down the road, a place to eat in with no frills about it of weeping, dancing, singing or writing messages on anything. And I discovered that it hardly mattered. Something must have purged itself on Amorgós last year. The need for weighing life in milligrams had gone.

One day when I was coming from the sea and being irritated by the other drivers on the road, I developed a special antipathy for a girl in front of me in a machine superior to her desert, and since all the cars on the road, apart from those weaving in and out, were going at the same speed in all lanes, I tried to force her over, and took at least five minutes in succeeding, by hooting and flashing lights, to pass her on the left. After a few miles I drew up in the left lane to turn at traffic lights, a sharp thud convulsed the car, a hit from behind that threw me forward in my seat, and I leapt out with a flood of agitated fury to pour down on the head of the girl whom I had passed. She had merely miscalculated half a metre, the lights were green ahead of her so she had supposedly been intending to go on. 'I haven't done anything,' she answered me with grumpy unconcern. Of the two of us it was she, who had offended, who was calm. She was right, however, in that she had done nothing to me but take me by surprise and hit my bumper hard. What filled me with truly bitchy pleasure was that she had dented the front bodywork of her own car, and since she did not bother to get out that would be her discovery when she got home.

'Athenian drivers!' I growled as I moved on, and that same evening, in the very same circumstances, felt the lurch again. This time it was a light one, the slow-motion meeting of two bumpers, and this time it was the driver in the rear who leapt out first. He was a young Dutchman and agonisingly upset. 'It's all right,' I assured him, 'you haven't done anything,' but I have seldom heard apologies so profuse.

Julia, Julia, I needed neither reassurance nor napkins, I did no mathematics of any sort. I drew some conclusions about the nationalities of different kinds of drivers, I drew no conclusion about the necessity for a third and worse crash from behind. Last year on Amorgós had its effect.

Thanks to Aiyiáli in general the process of living has become easier, and thanks to the Panayía specifically my autumn employment is moving into place. Again, I was helped at the Embassy before leaving Athens to make a decision for which I say now, frequently and fervently, 'Thank the Panayía!' The alternative might well have wrecked my life. That Virgin is going to have the fattest candle on her feast day that was ever lit by me in Greece. I light candles in churches for the sake of their icons, their caretakers or villagers. I shall light a candle to the Panayía for Langátha to which she belongs. If any visitors do come I hope it will be then, it is a dreadful day, but the Virgin will have her due in any case. She will have it on the Eve at the time of garlic shredding and that will be my saying of grace before Costa selects the tenderest goats' tongues.

CHAPTER SEVENTEEN

The Soup-Wrappers

I LIKE to organise my affairs so that occasionally I have a fulllength village day. I go down at about nine thirty if I have orchard lessons, towards midday if I have village ones, and coincide my up-coming from the harbour with sunset at the bottom and darkness at the top. But once a week I like to stay here, to know my house on one rare afternoon, to make positive rather than passive decisions about lunch and lie under my pine tree. On such a day I opened my first tin of piquant sardines from Katápola, and they were so piquant that even I, with the toughest foreign throat I know of, thought as at least two glasses of retsina were cancelled out with gasping that I might do well to turn the others in for two plain tins. So the *Chora*'s eggs and plums were redundant, the sardines were a hot mistake, and Sophia's mother, who arrived that night, often makes stuffed vine leaves fresh. Our own policeman can deal with a building permit, so that expedition may now be called a pleasure trip.

Having a day at home and emerging only for five minutes' shopping made me realise when I was suddenly breathless from writing in the evening how much I like Vassili and his wife. Here are quick-witted, good-willed, uncomplicated people, here is a shop where the thought, 'It is July and can I find a chair?' is simply ludicrous. The chair may be a step or a potato sack, but whatever form it takes no one who sits on it has any business obligation, either to buy or drink. Yet even in this easy atmosphere a change has taken place which I can only hope will fail to shake my faith in Greek spontaneity. Opening and closing times have been imposed.

'We can work,' Vassili explained, 'from seven to one, and in the afternoons from five to nine. Then I can't sell things any more, as a grocery this shop shuts down. I stay open only to serve drinks and then until eleven o'clock, eleven thirty on Sundays and festivals.'

'The farther from the beaten track you go,' I wrote, 'the farther you go from categories.' It is still true, but the road grows longer every year. At certain hours Vassili is a grocer and at certain hours a *cafenion* proprietor.

'And if the people have *kéfi*?' I asked. 'What if they have music and find the mood to sit until midnight?'

'Then they must get a permit. You can have a permit to sit late.'

'But if you suddenly have *kéfi* at five to eleven? Can you run to the policeman and get a permit then?'

Vassili smiled.

'It's getting like England,' I told him. 'Why go abroad to find your own country somewhere else?'

'It's for you,' his wife inserted, 'for tourism, to make the evenings peaceful for the foreigners.'

More mongrelism! Where is the latitude that was the mark of all Greek villages? I felt crushed and chilled. According to this, Vassili, Langátha has to shut down by eleven because of me. It usually shuts down by that time anyway, because it wants to. Who dares suggest that the villagers are unruly, that they disturb the peace of their one foreigner? And suppose — it is after nine o'clock now — suppose I should remember that I have run out of salt, that I have no fork to eat with, no paraffin for my stove, even that I am cold and need a sweater, for I hardly know what is not in Vassili's shop — the ceiling is a shelf crammed full — he with all these supplies dangling and overflowing and nothing much to do would have to deny me everything. One night last summer I smashed one of my lamps at ten o'clock and something must have been wrong with the other for it was my only source of light. I ran straight down to Vassili, as was natural, and came home immediately to finish work. Candles this year must be my only emergency supply, or else I must finish the evening in the dark.

All this time, while we sit over our retsina chatting, Vassili, whom I have never seen to drink one drop of alcohol, sits looking pleased with himself in a benign sort of way in his white jacket which is another new stipulation of the colonels, and in this case a pleasure to those inflicted by it — they would never treat themselves to such a thing but for the law.

'What would happen,' I asked him, 'if you served a drink and didn't put it on?'

'Clck,' he said, 'to Syra,' beaming, and the thought was so joyously out of keeping, that in this little grocery Vassili is so properly white-jacketed and would be criminally offending if un-white-jacketed that we almost defied the authorities by our joke. 'Take a photograph of me in it,' he begged, eradicating some of the irritation of his having to close down at the hour that he wants to anyway, to keep my peace.

Thus the evening's flippant pleasure in white jackets smoothed down my outrage over hours. It is still there, I am still outraged, but the impatient edges have been planed. It will take an inordinately long time to shift the character of Langátha, if not of Amorgós. Even in Athens, even in the heart of things, I go blundering ahead and usually find what I expect. In spite of military government the Litó Hotel continued to do curious and convenient things for me with unhampered cheerfulness.

Having arrived at the change-over of the seasons and thoroughly hot-showered on Spetsai, I was ready to return to the surroundings which I can afford from my own purse, retreating with a home-coming feeling to the Litó Hotel in Makriánni where I reclaimed my abandoned picnic basket from last year and sat on the same terrace in aerial spaciousness. I am rich, I can afford this terrace, it is the cheapest place in Athens apart from sordid cells, but as long as I have no shame in the choice for its own sake I am a millionaire. It is not the embassy, and every now and then the tap develops idiosyncrasies within half an inch of turning between being a dried-up fountain and a cataract, but what matter in a heatwave if you suddenly get splashed? The maids change my sheets not according to the amount of days I use them but according to their looks, which means — because of dusty feet despite all efforts — at least twice a week. My baggage is freely carried up and down whenever I go in or out, and that is continually; possessions that I leave behind are freely guarded or freely posted on; my habits — as near as I have any — are personally known, as are my plans, but known on the whole in the polite, the formal form. I ask for ice if I have visitors or am just hot and it is freely brought. I ask for breakfast, 'From what time can I have it?' — 'And four o'clock, and three o'clock if you like' — and it is freely carried up. Breakfast in higher-class hotels is 'from' a certain hour and then 'off'.

By 'freely' as I use the word I mean unquestioningly, as a pleasure, as part of work and life. Service is included in the bed-price, but that is low. I leave a moderate lump tip from time to time, for why after all economise on the poor, but it is less expected than deserved. One economises on the poor because it is easy, they are less demanding than the rich.

'And four o'clock, and three o'clock if you like.' I did not want my breakfast then but I liked to know the possibility. And another time I walked down to our neighbouring taverna with a sudden urge to add Russian salad to a picnic lunch and asked, 'Will you wrap me up a helping?' but foreseeing squashiness. 'And soup!' cried the head waiter. 'If you want it we will wrap up soup.'

It is such who are squeezed out by what is commonly called progress, half of which, like adaptability, is good. It is Irene in her enthusiasm for learning languages, it is an advance from earth closets that work to pipes that work as well. But I cannot see that anything is progress which means that supply ceases to co-ordinate with demand, when 'We have no time now' is the proud rejoinder to the question, 'How quickly can you mend my watch or make my dress?' If one is really progressing so that demand brings in more money than before one should have more employees and keep up the former rate. I broke my watch in Athens and it was repaired by the next day. I break my watch in England and it has to be sent off somewhere, thence probably to somewhere else, and the following week or the week after it comes back. If this is part of progress let me stay at the Litó, have three o'clock breakfast if I want it and wrap up my soup.

I think in any case that this would be an excellent idea: if I am ever technically speaking rich I shall keep up two hotel rooms, one A-class for the built-in comforts and one C-class for imaginative ones. The alternative is to be through the winter, then when the sun and sea take over, to be permanently ingrained with salt, but either way extremity is all. The middle Greeks are ashamed because their country is 'behind'. Shall I go out and tell them that they should catch up with central Europe by delaying over a repair to my wrist watch? Shall I tell them that their country is hideously riddled with night-time breakfasters, soup-wrappers, and jacks of all trades such as Costa and Michali Portokáli 'The Orange' on the quayside of Aiyiáli, Amorgós?

Michali Portokáli, a native of Thollária, is not in fact so much a jack of all trades as I had at first assumed, but when I took him to be one before I had sorted out the harbour characters he responded wonderfully. He ordered mules when I thought he was a muleteer, brought me fresh fish when I thought him — I am not sure what — and did all sorts of useful things before I realised that his business down there is a grocery, and having done so I saw no reason to stop calling upon his adaptability.

It is the peasants and ambassadors that are adaptable, and usually the middle men who make the laws. We had better stand by for another bunch of these: no jackery, no soup-wrapping, and no breakfast in the small hours, such things are 'behind' and it is the aim of governments to align their countries with everbody else. And after that may follow the introduction of a pair of snakes to Astypálaia.

But if Aiyiáli, which has led me into far extremes of living, submits to the smoothing of its own extremes, what will it have to offer to its visitors if my aim is realised and I give back where I received?

Total accuracy is almost impossible, especially in Greek villages, and my attempt towards it now is more of an admission of inability than a correction of the facts. I am bound to add a note here out of time that one evening in the first week of August our policeman accepted an ouzo at a quarter past eleven, outside, in the *platía*, and everyone joined in his leisurely discussion on whether we were making a public noise.

That is one fact, and another is that he had just exclaimed inside, 'But of course we can sit as long as we like in here, until one, until two, or talk all night if we are talking peacefully like this. Nothing has changed, but this is as before, you have to get a permit if you want to make a noise.' And then he banned an extension of the musical party from the *platía* to my balcony, and early the next morning when I woke rested and clear-headed I was pleased.

Yet the *magazí* which supplied him with the ouzo was the one where I had first heard the 'new laws'.

I doubt whether God himself could be entirely accurate about the villages, but I moved on to Vassili trying to do my best. 'What did I tell you, Carolina,' he said displaying a little notice on the door, 'what does all this mean?'

Grocery: weekdays, 7.0 a.m. – 1.0 p.m. & 5.0 – 9.0 p.m.
Sundays & festivals, 9.0 a.m. – 1.30 p.m.
Cafenion: weekdays, 6.0 a.m. – 11.30 p.m.
Sundays & festivals, 9.0 a.m. – 11.30 p.m.
Barber: weekdays, 7.0 a.m. – 9.0 p.m.
Saturdays: 7.0 a.m. – 1.0 p.m. & 5.0 – 11.0 p.m.
Sundays & festivals, 9.0 a.m. – 1.30 p.m.

I had obviously closed my eyes to that. It is black and white from the police station.

I have decided to avoid the danger of drawing general conclusions from all the evidence. I cannot replace my broken lamp at ten o'clock, when I can have my hair cut is the mootest point, I can drink with the policeman inside for the whole night, and there are opening and closing hours on Vassili's door. The only personal conclusion that I will draw is that I shall continue to have my bread buttered on all sides. I am left with enough outrage to prevent me from having to tear up my earlier pages; what remains may be preventative outrage against the future, and I need not go home at eleven o'clock. It is a great relief to know that we are not entirely deprived of latitude and sorted out.

CHAPTER EIGHTEEN

Karajoz v. Odysseus

THE shadow play of Karajoz has made its summer reappearance, with a nightly show in the *platía* for a week. The figures, nearly two feet high, colourful in patches where the light shines through the silhouettes and screen, are marvellously alert and mobile. 'Marvellous', like most of our 'awful' adjectives, has taken a declining path, but the performance is marvellous without decadence. Yerásimos Policrátos from Santorini, one of the forty-six remaining craftsmen-players in Greece still practising the art, a shoe-shine inbetween times, gives us a one-man show. Only when three figures appear behind the screen at once does he have any help, then twelve-year-old Vangeli holds whichever character is still. All the rest, two at a time in conversation, warriors, women, monsters, giants; fighting, loving, devouring each other, Yerásimos manipulates himself. He is all voices, male, female, animal, in speech and song, each different, and each funny, not as a quaint survival of the past, just plain funny. There is a wit and timing which through an amateur appearance is highly professional.

What fun the audience had. Here was George and the Dragon, Punch and Don Quixote in a Turkish background, injecting them with the most medieval of reactions, bawdy and humorous. Here was a good week's cinema-going, for the performance is not one; Yerásimos knows eighty-four works about the little, long-nosed Karajoz and six more 'of my own from my own head'. Truly, I felt, I am in Greece, even among this generous sprinkling of Turkish words which many of the children may not know, I am in a country which must not learn to be ashamed of what it is. This is their own, this is their inheritance, all that they have gathered from the days of Turkish occupation, all that they have received from the heroes of that time. They resisted and were liberated, why should they wipe out what proudly clings? We eat lamb and *kokkorétsi* roast on a spit and consider them a delicacy — why? The heroes in oppression stole the animals from time to time and roasted them on charcoal in the hills. They did not waste the guts but wound them up and put them in the embers too, and this is what we eat with relish while waiting to see Karajoz.

I always feel that Greece as a living country goes back to medieval days, and say so even though this year with repeated visits to its ancient sites my interest in antiquity has revived. A classical education leads one to expect stones and memories, a mingling with the people makes one more interested in life alive. After several years I have begun again to see the life in stones, and yet I do not connect this life with modern Greece beyond geography, I connect it with the world.

This summer I have brought along with me to Amorgós not only Julia and the Phengári, the people of Platí Yialó and Panagïtsa and all the Athenian driving-days, but Delphi and Mycenae too. Let my capacity grow, I want to reach out and draw back one peak experience of June: I am sitting at the top right-hand corner of the theatre at Delphi an hour before sunset when the rock is turning red. I am sitting petrified with the rock and thinking, 'If this is not one of the ten most beautiful sights of the world I have misconceived the capacity of the world, either I am seeing one of the ten most beautiful sights of the world or else the world surpasses what I think of it.' Like all great works of art it grows more moving, absorbs one further with familiarity, it is the history, not of Greece, but of us all. Once two eagles flew around the world and found the centre here. This stone is from the fourth century B.C., this from the fifth — what does it matter? I cannot bring myself to care. But down the road Oedipus killed his father and something happened at that moment which has changed our lives.

A party of schoolgirls on an outing jabber their way across the ruins of Apollo's temple as they come up merrily to test the acoustics of the theatre — something which can be done with dropping pins — resoundingly. It is theirs, it is ours, it is no longer a possession to be more than literally fenced off; the ancient past has been lost to the Greeks as their private property, they have the right to take the ticket money at the gate, they have the right to claim *kokkorétsi* and Karaïskakis as their own, they have the right, which I wish that they would claim, to be the people that they are. But Delphi is the centre of the world.

Delphi is the prelude to the Peloponnese and should always be so in the foreigner's grand tour, for then one follows the Sacred Way from Athens, rising through the mountains with every rugged piece of landscape seen by the ancient postulants to the oracle. The first view of the sanctuary is also the finer on approach from this direction, with no sight until one has passed it of the bric-à-brac modern town. And though Delphi is supreme, the Peloponnese can never follow as an anti-climax. Olympia may, but I think that is in its nature anyway; let it be the cool breathing-space between Delphic and Arcadian grandeur, a memory — and largely Roman — among pine trees. The ultimate goal is still Mycenae, and as such it can never disappoint but rather gains by all the superlatives that one has breathed before. Go to Bassae, go to Messene, go to Pylos, the longer the experience and the road the more one's understanding grows.

The road from Kalamata to Sparta is described by the *Blue Guide* as 'a grand scenic experience for those undismayed by heights'. This new English edition is a pleasure for its choice of words, in a succinct way they are suggestive as well as accurate. The range of the Taigetos has one pass and almost no habitation until an instant change takes place in style and colour, the mountains now are hard, severe in yellow-grey, and at this moment a notice by the road announces 'Sparta', a written word which seems to be redundant here for the scenery has done the announcing by itself. In one eyeful one knows what and why the Spartans were, a people who among these proud and brutal mountains led a proud and brutal life, who, enclosed between the Taiyetos and Mount Parnon exposed their babies, denied pleasure, lived not in families but regiments. 'What they were' was a basic piece of knowledge, but here we understand the 'why'. My small party has been struggling and enduring in Laconia; return into Arcadia soothes us, and on crossing Mount Parnon, travelling eastwards, we are like the Ten Thousand shouting, '*Thallassa!* The sea!'

One of the best-placed *cafenia* in the country has set its chairs and tables on this look-out post as if to ensure that anyone so careless as to drive past will be trapped into doing the right thing through fairly certain thirst. The plain of Argos, the richest plain in Greece, is spread beneath, how fertile, how kind and welcoming. And yet these attributes made it eventually more highly famed for bloodshed than Laconia — it was too desirable. Invaders, pirates, conquerors were merciless. Out there, after ten years' absence, the fleet from Troy came in, and with what relief of homecoming Agamemnon leapt ashore. That little hump which is Mycenae is the spot where Clytemnestra greeted him, as women greet their husbands, 'What you must need is a nice bath,' and when he had laid off his defences murdered him. The whole surrounding area is thoroughly hump-ridden; the Heraion where Agamemnon was elected leader of the Trojan expedition is apparent within walking-distance, and as near again stands Tiryns rivalling Mycenae's walls. There Heracles waited on the pleasure of King Eurystheus, performed his labours, and as a local hero ridding their neighbourhood of fear of wild beasts, grew in legend, was deified, and moved on to join King Arthur, Robin Hood and Davy Crockett in children's reading-books.

Nemea is out of sight around the corner, but the modern road which passes it is likely to mark the course down which he marched with the strangled lion slung across his back, and Lerna, plagued by the nine-headed Hydra, can be seen directly beneath us on the sea. His triumph over this part-immortal monster was a relief to the inhabitants of Argos too, a people who sent their own hero off to Troy, Diomedes of the loud war-cry, second bravest of the Greeks, who caused havoc among the gods. They suffered the same dangers, the same fears, as all the others of the plain, lived when Mycenae died, and now their Frankish fortress dominates one small area and is over-towered again by that of Nafplion across the bay.

History and legend, once diffuse, are packed into one view. But for the distance I would always approach the plain of Argos by this route.

Young Archilaus, known as Yorgo, at La Belle Helêne where Schliemann lodged when excavating the ruins of Mycenae, tells me, 'Every evening I walk up to the citadel, and in the summer I sleep out. I slept on the top of that mountain there last year, looking over Agamemnon's palace, and early in the morning I was woken up surrounded by a herd of gaping goats.' Archilaus, Nestor, Ajax, and Agamemnon and Orestes of the older generation all make good guides up there because they know their facts and their connection with the site is personal. But they are rare among Greek families in inheriting the ancient past themselves. One only has to travel once among the islands to see, for instance, how few have inherited their sea-faring constitution from Odysseus.

Athens today is hardly more than two hours from Mycenae by the modern highway. And now while the hectic days of preparation for Aiyiáli carry me in and out among ancient, modern, high and low, in a country taverna in an Attic village named Dhrosiá, which means 'cool', for the first time in a week we put our sweaters on. The sizzling of lamb spitting over charcoal is loud beside us in the night, and the son of the family brings us our plates head high. He says that he is eight years old, but if I can believe his aspirations he is seven going distantly on eight. Say that his parents could be fined in England, say they could be imprisoned, he is efficient, he is happy, he is Ganymede. The customers are spread among the trees throughout the orchard, dispersing his work among obscure and lighted spots. He runs and the paper table-cloths blow clattering behind him in the wind. The hungry come, and the paper cloths are sails, and they clatter and he is Ganymede.

So we say, and here we find him, but the discovery is ours, and Ganymede as much our own as the boy his parents' son.

Amorgós also has deep roots in antiquity which archeologists claim to be as ancient and important as on any of the Cyclades surrounding Delos, as is represented in Athens in the National Museum. But the roots of the people are in the monastery, in crumbling Byzantine churches, in the hills with icons miraculously found. Information that I might be given about earlier times would illuminate me no more than 'many many years'. Only in Athens I was sent out by an authority to rediscover Lila Marangóu, the island-born young archeologist whom I met last year in London, to educate me a little in the history of ancient Amorgós. It was she with whom I had had a *Chora* versus Aiyiáli exchange of conversation on the steps of the Savoy, a 'which of us eats *fava* more?' in a London taxi, who works now in the Benaki Museum in Athens, unable to leave the city long because of the need for reference books. But when it came to it, and we jabbered Amorgós enthusiasm over an encounter intended for the improvement of my mind, the outcome of the conversation was that her grandfather had been a pirate.

CHAPTER NINETEEN

Nikolaki's Lunch

I AM cross and fractious. I have spent a large part of the day being cross and fractious. That, without much provocation, was my reaction to 25 July. There must be a purpose in this so I lectured myself through clouds — the weather was despicable — on my way up. Find the purpose, it would be equally despicable to exhaust an evening's energy with daytime annoyances. If the most minor of events have reason this is it: I suppose that I only write at joyous hours, as if in a perpetually round-grinned state, the hi-di-hi hostess of a holiday camp, and all the joy of all these pages is quickly growing suspect without the rare confession of some fractiousness. So you've found your purpose, it's enough. 'Stop that,' I kept shouting to myself, aloud, on the mule track. Why add to some trivial inconvenience by making your head ache? Being cross and fractious is much more time-wasting than the thing which one is cross and fractious at. So go to the devil and shut up.

The happiness of Aiyiáli is not to be subdued by one day's headache, and I would hate it to be said — because it happened to coincide with a cross day — that I resent the orchard's new development. I have no reason to resent it, I am responsible myself. Niki the third and middle daughter has graduated to taking English lessons. On the morning when Irene had twenty sheets to wash and begged for a lesson in the afternoon it was inevitable, it was beyond control of my resolution to take no more pupils, that with a clear hour before me I should say, 'Send Niki.'

It was an innocent day three years ago when I suggested to

Michali that he might have a child who needed English lessons. He did indeed. And how his aspirations have been progressing since the machine began to work. Irene was twelve and had not seen the Latin alphabet. Niki at ten has been sent to the doctor since the winter to learn French once a week. This was the only foreign language going, but from the day this week when I said, 'Send Niki to me,' the French lessons have been cut. Michali must have had proper feelings since last Christmas about the possibility of excess and has even suggested paying me, a proposition right out of order in our system and quickly squashed. I replied that I meant to keep Niki's lessons to a minimum, a mere preparation for next summer after which she will join the Athenian ranks at grammar school. I wonder when eight-year-old Arguiroula will graduate? And Kianoula? But Irene will be a mother by that time with her diplomas on the shelf.

Her temporary period of motherhood is finished. Michali's wife returned thankfully to her *patrídha* from the foreign trials of Athens which proved no more than the price of reassurance about Kianoula's legs — they are pronounced no more than baby-bandy and basically all right. Irene can relax. I think that she enjoyed herself. She waited up at night for boats, the empty rooms turned into overflowing ones, those which they were building a week or two ago teemed for the first time with bikinified life, she looked after Greeks and foreigners, 'She's wonderful,' they said. Perhaps they did not know that she leapt up early in the morning to run up to Thollária — a rougher way than to Langátha and as long — to iron their sheets, cook lunch for whichever of the family was in the village and run down to cook in the orchard for the rest. The down-sheets went up for ironing and the up-sheets came down for washing, and *Jane Eyre* and gerunds were studied and absorbed. Then when the sweating midday moment came without the time to swim, when the ultimate justification for cross-and-fractiousness was reached, Irene would burst into my cottage smiling, 'But you know, I want to get thin.' She has bye-passed all the dangers of Athenian sophistication and adopted this piece only, one which gives her the ability to feel pleasure when the most forebearing of us might well sit down and weep. She is a little more womanly, it is true, but not to the extent where the vision splendid must be lost; she still has that.

Meanwhile a bewildering state of affairs has thrust itself into my life concerning the midday meal of Nikolaki, son of old Anápyros. He works most days in his orchard where we conducted our exchange of land among the fig trees and the butterflies, and of the produce which he brings up in the evening to Langátha one portion is cooked the following morning and sent down to him again. 'Who will take Nikoloas his lunch?' is a daily problem which has taught me what I feel to be half the relations of the village since the morning when I was spotted as obvious bearer of the billy-can. His wife, his mother, his mother-in-law and daughter all spend a piece of their morning's energy in sending each other, sending messages, am I going down today and at what time? If Nikoloas learnt how to cook himself and the beans had no return to make up and down the hill there would be much more simplicity in half a dozen people's lives. 'In Langátha everything is simple,' I wrote earlier, but rules have their exceptions. Everything is simple except Nikolaki's lunch.

Here we go now. Kyria Mouska, who is not my original Kyria Mouska but the widow of one-legged Anápyros, my friend who throws in herbs with cigarettes and goes on being cheerful in her weeds, accosts me first. Could I possibly pass by her daughter-in-law's house and collect the billy-can for Nikoloas? She makes herself indebted, but what are they to do? 'Come and drink a glass of wine this evening,' she calls after me as I comply. A little girl Sophia is next — it is unco-operative of her to have the name Sophia, but there it is and not inappropriate — arriving in my courtyard with a bag of beans. Do I want to buy them? That is an oddity. And will I pass by to take her father's lunch?

Sometimes it is the mother-in-law who comes, and she is Costaki's grandmother, the priest's wife, so I am more than ever connected with the priest. 'How is Costaki's English?' he can say now, 'And Nikolaki's lunch?' The lean, sad-featured woman, looking far more like a widow than the other grandmother, ventures, 'My daughter is cooking now, we would be indebted if you could pass by.... Is the boy coming for a lesson tomorrow? We must send you something.' My first offering from the priest's household was half a kilo of milk, produce which has not been seen in my kitchen since we used Jason's powdered baby-milk to make a batter for fried aubergine. Another time the message is sent up via neighbours and arrives distorted, 'You are to go to Costa's grandmother and fetch your lunch.' If I did not know which Costa and whose lunch this could lead to great embarrassment. And here is Sophia back again. Ten years old and curious she sits down at my table to watch me use my typewriter. Will I be passing to collect the billy-can? And she has brought me up two pillow-cases that I have had machined. Why certainly, but how is it that she is the bearer of these pillow-cases from material which I gave Yorgo's mother to machine? Yorgo's mother, I have learnt now, is Sophia's aunt.

But the deepest involvement in her relationships, and one that seems to me insoluble, concerns my old friend Marki who is sober when he cooks for festivals. He is a kind-hearted old man and I am fond of him however nearly he led to my disgrace in the *platía* in honour of the Holy Cross. He has had his trials of late, poor man, his right shoulder is in plaster, he has been in Athens for a month in hospital and keeping resolutely to doctor's orders in dry dock. Is alcohol bad for broken arms? But recently I rediscovered him at Yorgo's grandmother's *magazí*, the first that one passes coming up the village street, succumbing after seventy-seven abstemious days. 'I told the doctor,' he announced, 'that I would drink in secret.' He was certainly not doing so right then but was apparently informing us that secret drinking does no harm. And then the little Sophia came running down the steps, 'Drinking, are you, Granpa? Come back home.' And she stuck by him, until he finally succeeded in his shaking-off, with great stamina for a little girl sent out to retrieve her wayward grandfather. Her grandfather? So it was clearly said, and clearly verified, but in that case, if one grandfather is our late Anápyros and another the village priest she must have three. I would not put it past her. She is wise Sophia and she has three grandfathers.

'Is Nikoloas' lunch ready?' The messages still come, but I have taken to passing daily on my way down in any case. Half an hour later I am trudging past Michali's orchard through the intermittent bathers, dressed and hot myself. 'Where are you going, Carolina?' — 'I am delivering Nikolaki's lunch.' At first I could not even identify the man himself with certainty, for he is seldom to be found when I arrive. Then in the dim light among his mother's friendly tables I ascertained one evening that we were sitting face to face.

'What time do you like to eat?' I asked, for sometimes I wonder, when I come a little late, if it is hopeless hunger that makes him disappear. 'At ten,' he said, 'and three.' In that case whatever is his 'lunch' does not co-ordinate with my delivery. I call him through the fig trees arousing no answer but among the butterflies and hang the offering on the door. At some secret time it goes. Nikolaki is a satyr, and his daughter — now I can believe it — has three grandfathers. His wife's mother gives me milk, his mother gives me wine, and his wife gives me the opportunity to buy beans.

Nikolaki could not have been a reason for bad temper while it lasted, nor could the matter of another problem person in my life. The mayor's house is haunted. Maybe it is he himself who regularly waters the smallest lemon tree. Whoever it is is my domestic ghost.

The cold winter was a disaster for this year's citrus fruit. There is one big lemon on my major lemon tree, which I am guarding for some day's major emergency, one medium-sized, and several dwarfs. Costa, having long since picked the spring crop, is often in the courtyard watering, and a day or two ago he asked me, 'Did you water this little one?'

'Why, no, didn't you? The earth around the big tree was dry, and around the other wet. 'I never water it,' I said. 'I thought you did. It always looks like that.'

He stood still, working on the puzzle, and repeated, 'I watered them together the last time I came; this has been watered since. That's why I'm asking you, did you water it?'

'I never do,' I said. We shrugged our shoulders, 'Someone else....'

Someone else.... Someone else waters the little lemon tree, and since the damp earth has been brought to my attention I often notice that whoever it may be has been at work again. He has joined the daily infiltrators through my courtyard and it is kind of him.

I speak of 'my house' because I am in occupation and at home here, and 'my ghost' because he is attached, but the house is no more mine than he is, and the courtyard less than half of not being mine. Within the precincts of this mayoral seat — I often feel it to be as grand as that — I know all the independence and the ease of one who has full ownership, yet I belong to this house more than it belongs to me, I prefer to be part than to have it as my own. There is something else that I have been learning about Ulysses; he was not, as I once thought, presumptuous in his claim to partness, he made himself a gift.

So people on mysterious errands pass through 'my' courtyard. Let them pass. Adoni's wife and daughters are here again and may soon be among them, for this is Roussos property. Pupils, ghosts and Costa all come freely in, Nikolaki's womenfolk come with their messages about the billy-can; until last year, when the well failed, some of my neighbours used their water rights; once the gate banged open and a little girl dashed in, fled under one of the arches, squatted throwing up her skirt, and dashed out again relieved. During the last day that I spent entirely up here I found one of the villagers surveying the outhouse on the far side of the courtyard, standing on the roof and peering, 'I'm going to have this one repaired. I'll do it with Costa, half and half, because I put my animals in here.' Does he? I have never noticed them. Or perhaps they are to be my new visitors from now on.

Apart from all these incursions of neighbours and relatives I understand that my courtyard is a right of way through to the fields up above. This preserves a link with my original Kyria

Mouska, who must have goats or beans or something on this side, for she often comes. It only means that nearly every day one person or another passes and I am preserved from thinking that I have a castle in this house. It only means that I cannot sunbathe in the nude, and I do not want to anyway. How, if I did, could I recognise from the shape of a small bikini that the sun and I are still in touch when I take a bath in an English February?

I feel exorbitantly in touch with everyone today. Hullo, world, I want to shout, so you have caught me up. It is Sunday, on Sundays communications operate, they have come over the mountain, they have come over the sea, there were four letters for me in the home office of Langátha and two came to the orchard, to the very door of my cottage with the postman in the middle of siesta time. That really is exorbitant and must be stopped.

Henry wants to build, Henry is undeterred by babies, perhaps he realised that — unless Catherine should confound us all with twins — we shall have enough backs for the hill and none of next year's loads will be too great. I am to go into action, producing builders' estimates, facing the moment that has been creeping up on me of offending the builder that I am supposed to hire, facing the further distant moment when I may offend a carpenter. I may be wrong, I may be hard, but right now my firm opinion is that no desultory greetings over friendly glasses are going to influence the matter of employing craftsmen for this house. Being inescapably escorted to Karajoz will not move me. The expectation of widows and grandmothers will not come into it. Possessions may lead to trouble but this will be no more my own house than the mayor's, and I rather suspect that so long as my motives and decisions have sense in them, — usually Costa's which leads me among reliable Langátha men — no one's sensible relations will take offence. The word is largely out of keeping here. And, 'Have you had any dealings with the Anápyros heirs?' writes Henry. Yes, I can answer, I have intimate dealings with the direct heir himself, and with his butterflies. It never occurred to me, so slowly minds can move, what ambassadorial work the billy-can performs.

None of these letters heralded an arrival at Aiyiáli, from the mainland or from Mykonos. The scheme has broken down this year but I am far too occupied for loneliness and cannot feel abandoned since I did the abandoning myself. The *tachidrhómos* is bringing another pillow on the boat, but never mind, the Barretts can lay their heads on it when they come for the festival, and they had better have a comfortable night. Then I shall inform the Panayía when I light the candle which is due that my debt is not forgotten but repayment will have to be postponed. There may even be some interest if I can manage that.

Candle-lighting was one of the intense subjects of discussion in Anápyros' and Vassili's shops at the end of last September when I was doing too much discussing too wildly because I should not have been there. 'Do you go to church?' they asked. Why, no. I meet so many different sorts of people, I travel so much, and in a Muslim country too, how am I to know that this or that is right? How can I think that one right way exists? They, a church-going people, but not feeling their own faith to be attacked since they do not do these things themselves, asked, 'What do you believe in then?' and I answered, 'A good heart.' It sounds much better as *kalí kardhiá* in Greek, it would have sounded better still coming from one of them, not me, but it fell like sense among them and they also said, 'That is a good belief.'

During a bad period this was one incident in which I had no shame. The simplicity of believing in a good heart annihilates the need for generations of theological works, or so I felt, and it seems perh aps a little presumptuous to knock them over from the mayor's house or from the orchard with one blow, but I remembered the scene vividly today, it was revived by letters from more sophisticated realms, and I thought, if there is goodness in Aiyiáli — and I see it — and if I speak in the terms of its own simplicity, then I see no reason to aim higher than to believe in a good heart.

CHAPTER TWENTY

The Siege

I HAVE come in with one of the heaviest baskets yet carried up the mule track to stand a twenty-three hour siege. It is ten to nine, 30 July, and I shall emerge tomorrow at the beginning of the non-hour, which is twilight, not just because I have to meet two builders to hear their estimates but because it is essential at that time, in any circumstances, to emerge. It is the hour, if not for walking, for sitting with no book and perhaps no conversation on one's balcony, the inbetween time for passive taking-in, when it is still too early to light lamps, too dark for indoor detail, and the people wait for night to be complete. But I call that moment the beginning of the following day, and the next hour of void its end, a working habit which still depends upon the sun. Thus my days start in the evening and finish on the morrow an hour earlier; I preserve the time of nothingness and privately my dates work from the end to the beginning of each twilight.

There are long eras and little eras even in continuous living. This, for no particular reason, is the ending of a little era, July is closing down and when the siege ends we shall be four hours from August. That is coincidental, let us rather say that the belated grapes will have ripened when I come out — let us fix the ending of this era on the grapes. They will be ripe in the plain and I shall receive my first bunch in the orchard, but shall I receive it from Costa through the cottage window or from Michali through the door? Then the Panayía will have her day and then it will be autumn. I have decided to stop here. When I emerge and there is more to say I will not say it. Vangeli and Michali will come early in the morning for a lesson, and then Yorgo, and I will pour boiling oil on intriguing trivialities. If Costa comes I will not talk about the moon. I will withhold the astronauts from him until my final word is typed.

Certainly the moon-walkers have nothing to do with the ending of this era. When I gave a list of orders to the *tachidhrómos* last week and added as an unpremeditated superfluity, 'And a Sunday newspaper,' writing down a list of names to be displayed at any central kiosk, it did not occur to me that if he were to carry out that errand it would bring news of the first landing on the moon. We are not inordinately interested in it here. Over lessons and in Vassili's shop I have mentioned, 'My family in England watched the first foot being set upon the moon,' and that sounded much more unlikely than the setting of the foot itself, and quite unreasonable. Costa will have an opinion on the matter, the rest of us are more inclined to think only what boulevards could be constructed through the island at that price. I am not going to wait for Costa's saying, I am not going to wait for goats' teeth from the policeman, nor builders' estimates, nor visitors. I am certainly not going to wait for any road. They may or may not happen, life will go on and I shall finish chattering with my siege.

Rather than suggest to the *tachidhrómos* that I have thousand-drachma notes flowing about my purse, I got Vassili to break one before I paid my bill, and rather than suggest to Vassili — however much I like him — that such notes flow I made a point of saying, 'There goes August's portion and it is still July.'

'Do you need one thousand a month?' he asked. 'A dollar a day, do you need that?'

It did seem rather extravagant. But I smoke too much, you know, Vassili, and I drink wine, you know that too. I buy very little food but there is always something — if not to eat then paraffin or stamps. Stamps cost three eggs each for a one-page letter to my English home. A dollar a day is only just enough.

I felt almost apologetic in my defence, but afterwards I did not feel apologetic to myself. It is good to feel the dollar valuable again. Each article has twice the value where we pay twice as little — we respect it more. Sophia knocks at my cottage door while I am eating a lunch of *bámyes*, the beans which we call 'ladies fingers' for their pointedness, and comes in with a boiled egg. 'My mother sent this because the *bámyes* were so tough,' and yet the sauce was excellent; I recognised the pride of a good cook. One drachma here may be five or ten in Athens, but that its calculated value gives more pleasure to the spending. Here we are scrupulous but not finicky. *Bámyes* are difficult to cook; I call them scratchy, others call them slimy, and Sophia's mother, not being satisfied, sends me a boiled egg.

So I have paid my small bill to the *tachidrómos* with the sense of giving and receiving riches, and am being impressed now by that native wit which leads him to decisions which are usually fortunate. It must be native wit for I sometimes think he does not understand much Greek, let alone a foreign script. There was not another pillow in Athens, he informed me, such as he had brought before and in anticipation of which I had got Yorgo's mother to machine the case. How far did he search? And he judged the alternative too expensive so he properly refrained. Since my visitors do not arrive why should I need another pillow? The Barretts can share one after all. But he did bring lemons, and although they inevitably coincided with our first load from Naxos one can never have lemons in excess. He did bring me the negatives of the two films that I have taken, which reassures me that I have learnt how to use my camera, and he did bring me a second copy of the new English book that I am using with Michali and Vangeli, but when I asked, 'And did you find a newspaper?' he simply threw back his head.

'What would you want with newspapers?' I took him to respond, and I suspect myself of feeling some relief. The English book is our life's blood, those two who have finished one's year's reading despite a ten-month holiday and been rewarded with a bonus of the auxiliary 'do', would never be denied the next step in their progress by a senior islander. Meanwhile whatever is going on outside goes on, and unless something so momentous happens in the world that even the inhabitants of Aiyiáli let me know, or someone sends a telegram, I shall not help by reading newspapers. No one has sent me any telegram so far this year; Miki, who has even given up receiving letters, has had all his problems solved.

I think perhaps I should have been a *tachidhrómos*. You spend a week in Athens thinking; what a bumble jumble, involving your mind with curious decisions, and then a week in island isolation thinking, 'Thank God for peace and quiet, blessed *isichía*!' I think perhaps I *am* a *tachidhrómos*, I think it a good thing to be, I would rather be one than, say, operate a lift. Life so far as I know it is a succession of antidotes between extremes; perhaps that is not to be recommended but on the other hand what is life but a fulfilling of errands, a fetching and carrying? There are so many interesting things to carry back and forth. Nikolaki's lunch is one of them.

Walking down the beach and delivering the billy-can I meet one of the few annual Aiyiáli foreigners and we talk a little and eventually he says — he's bound to say it — 'What do you do?'

What do I do? I am taking Nikoloas his lunch and I shall hang it up among the butterflies. 'But what do you do?' he asks. I am doing what I am doing, the tense you use confounds me utterly. I am living in the mayor's house, I am living on Mykonos, I am driving out of Athens, and I divide my living into chunks and have all of them at once.

That 'What do you do?' being largely a financial question, prevents me from saying that I teach the children, it almost prevents me from saying that I am a writer, it excludes me from from nearly all my doings, yet I earn what I spend and I live. I do not believe that I am an exception, I think it disastrous if I am, because then my dislike of 'What do you do?' must also be exceptional and people think that living is finance. Yet, 'What do you do?' they ask.

The sun is hot on Platí Yialó, and I am sitting at Marina's taverna in the shade, and plunging into the sea, sitting at Yorgo's and then at Petinos'. 'Are you on holiday?' On holiday from what, I ask you, on holiday from life? My head is aching from hours of translation, hours at Marina's, hours at Yorgo's, hours at Petinos', words and words and words. But I am at those places while I am writing them, and that is doing too. I am translating *Lady Chatterley's Lover* into English, I cannot for the life of me think why, I am translating a stage play 'based on the homonymous novel by David Herbert Lawrence' and it pays for Mykonos. So you are a translator? That is what you do. But I am sitting at Marina's, Yorgo's and Petinos', must I exclude that? And am I to exclude talking on the quayside in the evenings, confusing and unconfusing minds with argument, the discovery of barnacles? Am I to exclude picking mulberries? They leave my working body, even in an old shirt of Yanni's, as stained as any labourer's. Am I to exclude loving? I walk from the village after midnight and sleep for four or five hours in that other orchard cottage, dreaming, and then it is the morning and the day begins again. Which of those hours must I exclude? What do you do? — I live. Where do you live? — In the world.

Water ripples over sprawled-out ankles on the sea's edge around Cape Sunion. Say, if you like, this expedition is financed so this is work. Say this if you like, lying beneath a pine tree at Skiniá, hugging Julia in the early hours, talking nonsense to a taxidriver; say this, if you must differentiate, preparation for Amorgós is work. It is totally exhausting, allow that to justify the word. But do not dare to say that I am 'gathering material'. That is the only thing I do not do. I am sitting at the top right-hand corner of the theatre at Delphi, I am translating *Lady Chatterley's Lover* into English, I am taking Nikolaki his lunch, I am looking at Ganymede. To work is to play is to do is to play is to work. Where do you live? I live.

Yul Brynner, so the *Athens News* informed us in the early summer, was to make a film on Mykonos, hiring as extras all the donkeys of the island and of Delos, to advertise some German tobacco company. 'What do you do?' they say. Ask the donkeys of Delos what they do.

It is ten to six, the sun is lowering and there are two more hours to this day which is now July the thirty-first. I shall go out when I am ready, I shall open the gate at whatever hour I have finished and the purpose of my siege will have been served. What would become of discipline if rules and regulations, laws and personal decisions did not have a certain latitude? We would lose the right to exert our self-control. I shall do what I shall do and then go out. I have been out already, I went to buy some pepper at midday. Call that cheating if you like to work by rule of thumb. I walked once around the village, but privately I remained within my siege.

I am looking forward to going out again. I am looking forward to hearing news from builders and achieving an inoffensive relationship with each. I wish that I were staying ten days longer and could look forward to Stavró, I want to be here for that little festival and dance in the *platía* on the Eve. I can understand about wrongness and learn too without being pompous, when I have *kefi*, about bans.

I think that I have solved both ghost and grandfathers, but never mind.

There is a lizard in my cottage who needs to solve himself. He keeps returning for the sake of looking pale and lost to exactly the same spot at the top corner of the wall. But since he has the energy to climb so high and knows which spot to come to he cannot be pale and lost.

Phaní should be our next arrival in the village, and possibly he and Costa will sleep up here again, though I think that the family house below has beds large enough for all. Pepi likes the middle best, she says, when they are three.

I must remind the two Sophias and Irene not to go putting Athens into a compartment any more and to take their swimming-suits when they go back.

Two little girls, this moment, have run up on to my balcony, reminding me that I do not have a castle after all. I say on one page that I do not have a castle and on the next that I am going to stand a siege; human beings are indefatigably illogical. I am glad about that on the whole. I turned out the girls severely because they were neither watering lemon trees or flagstones, using a right of way nor bringing messages, and I was in the middle of a thought. Yet they reminded me. Having no castle I shall go out when I want.

The only thing that worries me is mice. I thought that they had come back, but I must have done so in a dream. This is another reason for leaving a place such as Langátha at the right time; dreams become so vividly domestic that sooner or later one cannot know who has said what, and which thing — in waking hours — is. I do know that I have not seen one spider here this year. I know that I have had ants twice and thwarted them, but I wish that there were a poison which only rats would eat, I would rather not thwart mice so painfully.

And I have an owl. How, speaking of my nightly noises, could I forget my owl? But I am Faust at midnight and, owl, poor owl, the time is running out.

This piece of timing is coincidental, but very soon the battle of the Virgin's doodles will begin. One day, or never, the celebrators of her festival will come by car.

Why wait until the fourteenth? After such a sedentary day I could walk into the country and light her candle now. I should have time to go and come before tomorrow, which will begin with builders in an hour and a half. There is time and I will go.

'When shall we dance again?' calls my skinny friend Adoni on the quayside. When shall we dance? We shall.